A Throttled Peacock

For Karen & Minzen

all best.

Also by C.W. Smith

Thin Men of Haddam
Country Music
The Vestal Virgin Room
Buffalo Nickel
Uncle Dad
Letters from the Horse Latitudes: Short Fiction
Hunter's Trap
Understanding Women: A Novel
Gabriel's Eye
Purple Hearts: A Novel
Steplings

A Throttled Peacock

Observations on the Old World

Essays by

C.W. SMITH

De Golyer Library
Southern Methodist University / Dallas

First edition
ISBN 978-1-878516-09-1
Printed in the United States of America
10 9 8 7 6 5 4 3 2 1

To Marcia
Wing to wing / Oar to oar

Contents

Foreword IX

Getting To Know You 1
When your only friend becomes your worst enemy

A Franco-American Etiquette Brouhaha 13
Learning that all manners are local

A Postcard from the Algarve 21
My fears secretly walk me to where they can see themselves

The Kindness of Strangers 27
Considering the necessity and danger of trust

Learning Inefficiency 57
Local customs provide needed therapy

Views of the English at Oxford 65
Wondering if Mother really knows best

Home On the Range 79
Encountering a specter of homelessness

The Folks at Café d'Angleterre 107
A longing to be known becomes a potent force

Foundlings 119
*When the glorious past bumps up against
the prosaic present*

We Teach the French About Texas Chili, Sort Of 129
Culinary hubris leads inevitably to humiliation

Night Train 139
A new experience unearths an old memory

In Praise of Stone: 149
Humble materials take on a new perspective

About the Author 159

Foreword

Although the experiences I describe in *A Throttled Peacock* all occurred while I was traveling, this memoir of sorts isn't a travel guide — I have no recommendations to make about food, lodging, or transportation. I've sought rather to record the psychological, emotional or intellectual shifts that have come from being estranged from my usual life, by being there where nothing seems the same, there where new feelings and notions arise from being in new locations. Traveling in foreign countries inevitably — if not compulsively — encourages comparison and contrast and calls on dormant parts of your psyche the way using new weights in a gym results in new aches and pains but also new strengths. That's what my focus became in writing about these experiences: what new ways of looking at my world and myself startled their way into my consciousness when I was there where I am a stranger?

Some of these pieces were published elsewhere, and I want to thank the editors of those magazines and periodicals for their generosity. "Getting To Know You" and "A Franco-

American Brouhaha" appeared in *Hemispheres;* "We Teach the French About Texas Chili, Sort Of" appeared in *Texas Monthly*; "Views of the English at Oxford" was in *Pembroke*; and "In Praise of Stone" was published in *Texas Architect.*

Getting to Know You

*When your only friend becomes
your worst enemy*

Searching for the flower clock in the *Jardin Anglais*, I think of nifty ways to kill my wife. Maybe force-march her barefooted over Siberian tundra while prodding her with a stick, since she seems to feel that's what I'm doing now.

"It's cold," she whines. "We've been out all day long!"

All day? It's 3:30, and we didn't start until 9:37. We walked to the *Palais de Nations* — okay, farther than I promised, the weather colder than expected — but I paid by returning to the room for 11:00 tea and a rest (she rested, I drummed my fingers). After lunch, we browsed in book shops in the *Vieille Ville*, saw the *Petit Palais* Museum, then hiked to the park off the *Place Neuve*, where chess players moved knee-high plastic pieces. I marched us over to the *Musée de l'Horlogerie et de l'Émaillerié*, where Marcia sat in the foyer while I studied a chiming clock that dramatized the Annunciation with wooden figures.

Then I agreed to go "home." My map said we'd pass this "flower clock," but we've been weaving around the garden facing a stiff wind off Lake Leman, and ... no clock!

"It's over there." I point toward home; it's a ploy.

"You don't really know."

She won't navigate but criticizes when I do. "Do you want to see the map?"

"No, I want to go home. We've been looking for hours."

"We'd be there if you wouldn't drag your heels."

"I'd feel more like hiking if you'd walk beside me instead of in front."

If I break my stride to fall back, she'll slow to a stop, protest by dawdling.

"Why do you care about this flower clock?"

"It's famous."

"I've seen enough famous stuff today. Let's go."

What if Peary had listened to the whiners? "Suit yourself. But I didn't come halfway around the world to watch TV, for God's sake."

She halts; her lower lip curls. Any second, she'll snuffle. A bystander wouldn't know how keen a cut "TV" was. We have a running debate about popular culture; she can actually watch "Entertainment Tonight" without puking and dislikes chess because it's "war-like." She'd rather stroll through a French supermarket than a cathedral, and she doesn't like chamber music because it has no lyrics.

"That's a cheap shot!" Her voice trembles. "How much TV have I seen the past four months!?"

The question's rhetorical; our hotel here's the first with TV we've had. But if virtue's sole guardian is the unavailability of temptation....

The Grand Exit's next — she neatly faces about and marches to the Hotel Tor and its steaming radiator and American TV shows.

I won't chase her. I'm going to bag this flower clock if it kills me. She'll have to tell people she was watching some ancient rerun of "Happy Days."

We're not our normal selves, I swear. Here's our usual us: once I saw a documentary about an elderly English writer and his wife. They had that peas-in-a-pod look of ancient marrieds, just alike but for hats and height. With only two good legs between them, they leaned on matching canes and walked shoulder-to-shoulder; from a distance they looked like an A. One was deaf and the other blind. Evenings, the deaf one read aloud to the blind one. Except for that, "We haven't spoken to one another since the Blitz," said the writer. "Have a spat?" asked the astonished interviewer. No, said the writer, "Just telepathic."

Normally we talk things out and reach agreement readily. Among our friends, we're famous for not bickering. Our kitchen choreography's Broadway precise. On walks we turn however the world has thwarted or pleased us into words for one another's hearing. Our best TV's in our bedroom so we can lie in one another's arms to watch; the best part of our day is right before we fall asleep together.

But traveling has curdled the milk of togetherness. Now we're like two countries with a common border that lived harmoniously until a change of government brought jingoistic new regimes bristling with suspicion.

Earlier in our trip Marcia went shopping with a new acquaintance in Madrid while I read in a cafe. Those hours alone felt like a vacation. She returned much too ebullient. She said, "It felt good to be off the leash."

Of course she exaggerated. But you wonder — can being in nonstop proximity make even my beloved spouse yearn to slit my throat?

They say you should spend an hour alone for every day you're traveling with a companion. We're now on day 125, and we've accrued an eighty-hour backlog of therapeutic solitude. It gets to you, having to share tiny spaces; every place you turn, someone crowds you, and it's always the same old one. *What? You again?*

When I sneeze, Marcia mutters, "Should have brought your allergy medicine." My elbow's in her face when we eat side by side. And speaking of elbows, she gripes that I always take the common armrest. Also she claims that my new habits of daily wine and cigars make my snoring a lot worse; she used to tap me lightly to turn me over, but now she hollers in the dark, "Quit snoring!"

Sometimes she'll gaze out a train window for hours to keep from having to look at me.

"What're you looking at?" I ask to torture her.

The syndrome where you crave the thing you're allergic to sets in, so you can't resist doing whatever's most annoying. If she gets out of bed at 2 a.m., I say, "Where you going?" When she ignores me, I say, "Where are you going? Huh? Huh? Huh?" until she screams, "WHERE DO YOU THINK!!" Then I act hurt. "Jeez! No need to bite my head off!"

Recently she asked, "You know what I don't like the most about you? You have to make all the decisions."

I protest. Being a control freak and traveling with another one for months without a fixed itinerary presents infinite opportunities for argument. Imagine "thermostat wars" mul-

tiplied by a hundred. Where and what will we eat for breakfast? What time will we go out? Where should we eat lunch?
What shall we do first, second, or not at all? What city shall
we visit next?

Originally, we divvied up the labor, but I forget what she
was to do. Most things are on my shoulders — changing money,
planning routes, deciphering the Thomas Cook book of rail
schedules, locating banks and tourist bureaus, schlepping
bags, negotiating with cab drivers, ticket agents. Traditional
boy stuff.

I feel sorry for myself. Why do I have to do everything?
She'll argue that meals, laundry, and hotels are her domain.
But then each meal requires delicate negotiations; my propos-
als are rejected one by one until I say, "Okay, you decide." What
she wants to eat is: 1) right this instant; 2) clear across town or
the Atlantic; 3) nothing because she feels too fat.

This isn't normal, either. At home we maintain the house-
hold without much regard to gender. Traveling has regressed
us to "I Love Lucy" stereotypes. She has become The Spoiler
— she wallows in that infantile state where you go limp in the
supermarket aisle and scream bloody murder if you don't like
what mother's chosen for you. She claims I'm The Bully.

This world-famous flower clock — I find it two hundred
steps from our spat. The face is subdivided into quadrants
composed of colored flowers, and long, slim metal hands move
above the beds.

But I don't care. Spotting it, I felt a tiny thrill of discovery,
but then it was *seen one, seen 'em all*. Shivering, I stare as if it
might do something to justify my tracking it down, or at least

justify our fight; I stare so people will think I'm a serious looker, and not a fellow who'd forcemarch his wife across Geneva on a freezing afternoon to see a boring flower clock that could be fully appreciated by the briefest glimpse from a tour bus.

The icy wind cuts short my pretense of interest in this stupid flower clock (Good Lord! Do the Swiss make clocks out of everything?), so I stride down to the *Promenade du Lac*, hurry by the docked excursion boats empty and rocking in the wind. On this late wintry afternoon, the sun is a pearl button behind a gauze of high cirrus; the wind sweeps away its pale white light. Men in topcoats clutch their lapels and hold down their hats. I turn up my collar, and the tips sting my cheeks.

In an almost deserted tea-shop I sit at a table beside the front window. My ordered tea arrives in a big metal pot with a pitcher of cream and a saucer of sugar cubes.

Ah, alone at last! But as minutes pass, I can't enjoy my solitude. I feel self-conscious. My toes twitch. Stack sugar cubes, unstack them. I mentally record this (I am stacking the sugar cubes) as I do it. I peer out the window. My gaze caroms about as if repelled by any surface it strikes.

My knack for being alone, my contemplative self, has withered; the part of my nature that aggressively procures food, shelter and transportation has been pumping iron, and I'm muscle-bound. Jaded by over-stimulation, I have the attention span of a hyperactive ten-year-old. Soon as we step off a train and wrestle our room and scout out our restaurant and recon for the bank and the tourist office and cruise the Top Five sites, I'm itching to roll again. My plotting brain is always casting a city or two ahead of where the rest of my body is, and when *there* turns into *here*, I hardly know what to do.

If I don't make our decisions, what will I do? All this time I imagined they were a means to an end, but now I see they've become the way I define my self.

I come out of the shop into a violet dusk. Stores are closing. Cars stream by with lights on; men and women in trench coats trudge uphill toward the train station with briefcases and shopping bags, blank faces bathed in a ghastly, Edward Hopper aura.

The lingering light casts a security-lamp hue over the city, making of upper windows shimmering, molten-silver surfaces. Blown wrappers, rare on Geneva streets, swirl up, carrying a hint of bad weather. Sure hope not. We don't have much protection from it.

I think Marcia bolted partly to avoid being out at the close of this chilly, windblown day. To be a tourist at twilight gets her down. She's a homebody; in the winter, she loves to change right into sweats soon as she's home from teaching and to take a supper of waffles to bed while lying under her down comforter and working the New York Times puzzle.

If Marcia were here, she'd say, "Everyone else is going home." She'd imagine pots simmering on glowing burners, steamed-up bathroom mirrors, deerskin slippers, kids doing homework while drinking cocoa from mugs.

At first she could work long days as a tourist without much down time, but now, after four months on the road, she's much less able to stand the omnipresent foreignness and the bitter weather outside our rented rooms. The cold has become a psychological condition. "I wouldn't mind the cold so much if

I knew I could eventually get warm," she often says. She means that if she could go home at the day's end then she wouldn't get depressed. She grew up army-brat uprooted, so sometimes ghosts of that early transience shake her bones. I stayed put from the second grade to graduation, so roving about the globe is making up for lost time.

So it falls to me to be the rock. Usually I am. But on a day like this, when I'm cold and my feet hurt and I'm thousands of miles from anything familiar, I envy these homeward bound Swiss, too.

What I have, still, is her. And at least at the Hotel Tor, I can find my only friend in Europe, and though two's a tiny unit, having one other person who knows you well feels like a club or a family when you're surrounded by a million strangers.

Losing each other has been our greatest fear. We worked out elaborate contingency plans in case, say, I stepped off a train and she didn't, and in each new town we name a place within the station to go to if we lose each other later.

Walking alone in the chilly twilight, I see now that what we haven't done is to plan to be apart. The moral? If you don't arrange to have time apart, you'll pick fights to get it. Then you spoil your solitude stewing.

It would be sad to tramp about in this bony dusk heading for an empty room. Not all these citizens have best friends — they may live alone or with people they don't want to see. So I'm a lucky guy. Seeing ten thousand flower clocks wouldn't equal fifteen seconds with my soul mate.

To make amends, I buy a log of Toblerone chocolate. Then, in the lobby, I consider my entrance to room 304. I can get a key at the desk or knock for Marcia to let me in. When you're fighting, even something this simple has ramifications. Letting myself in suggests: 1) I'm ashamed, and I didn't want to trouble you; or 2) I'm not about to ask you to do anything for me.

On the other hand, knocking might say: 1) I'm humbly asking permission to enter your exalted presence; or 2) I'm still the injured party so you can damn well open this door. Knocking drags the other party instantly to the bargaining table. And what do you reply to a snarly, "Who's there!"

Could try cute. Who's there? *Ben. Ben who? Ben Missinyou.*

To keep my options open, I get a key, and, outside our door, I cock my ear, hear nothing.

I go tap tap thinking I'll try an "It's me" that sounds like the same old worthless fellow, but no one says *Who's there.* Shower? No rushing water. If she's napping, another knock will put me way behind in subsequent negotiations.

I use the key, crack open the door, stick my hand through and waggle the Toblerone bar. No response. I go in, scan the room. It's empty. And dark. I hit the overhead light, but the illuminated contents say little as to her whereabouts, her mood, her intentions. Her blue L.L. Bean bag lies by the bed, her cosmetics pouch still perches on the basin, so she didn't pack. The bed's been made, so I'd guess she didn't nap. I set my palm on the top of the television set, since I once saw a detective on TV do that. It's cold. Surprise.

I turn on the television. BBC News. I lie on the bed and absently absorb the flickering images. She might have gone to the nearby theatre that shows recent American films, but she would've left a note, even if we're quarreling. She wouldn't want me to worry about her. That's not a game we play.

If she collapsed on the way back or was struck by a car
and went into a coma, could anyone reach me? We're *sans* cell
phones, and normally we each carry our hotel's business card,
but did she have one today? How about her passport?

I rummage through her bag; her travel wallet's gone, so
she's wearing it. That's a relief; at least, authorities could learn
her name and address.

But what if she's been kidnapped?

I continue with this awhile — slave traders, terrorists, etc.
— but eventually my stomach growls. I could eat the Toblerone.
If something's happened to her, I'll need my strength. And if
she's kidnapped or comatose, she won't need a chocolate bar.

Nobly, I resist. Instead, I think about what a tragic figure
I might become, the object of friends' efforts to help me forget
my sorrow. But no sooner do I warm to the benefits of being a
widower than I hear my wife rising from the dead at the door.
She's using her key. I wonder what it means.

"Ward, you're home!" I declare. "I was worried!"

She laughs; she's carrying a small plastic bag.

"I've been out exploring. It's not nearly so cold out there
when I'm choosing to be out in it."

"Well, here's your reward." I offer the candy bar.

"Awww..." We embrace. Then we sit side by side on the
bed, and she pats my knee. She doesn't remove her coat, scarf
and beret.

"So how was the flower clock?"

I consider lying. I'm not above it, understand: it just
wouldn't serve my purpose now.

"Sucks green boogers, *amiga*. I'll find a postcard and that'll
be all you need to know."

"Well! Now aren't you sorry you tortured me over it?"

"Sure. But it might have been terrific."

"Not likely. Get your coat."

"Why?"

"Don't argue. I've decided that my trouble is that I've let you decide things so I can reserve the right to complain. And I know that's not fair."

"Where are we going?"

"Just do what I say. You won't need a map, either."

"Is it a restaurant? Because I'm hungry, aren't you?" (Turns out she does lead us to a marvelous cafeteria — great strawberry tarts!)

"You'll find out."

Outside, the wind's less ferocious, and the night is starred with street lamps, display windows striking up the band with footlights, mannequins posed for a show just after the curtain has gone up.

She hums "Follow the Yellow Brick Road" and takes my arm the way you do when you're pulling, not hanging, on your partner; I will myself to let her bully me into doing as she says. I'll be free to congratulate or to blame her. These are novel options, and I look forward to exercising them.

A Franco-American Etiquette Brouhaha

Learning that all manners are local

Irene, the cook, has gone on strike. A curtain of beads divides her kitchen from the terrace where we several Americans, a couple of Brits, a Dane, a Finn, and an Italian have been called to assembly, and we can see her pacing and muttering in her domain.

The problem? It seems, says Simone the translator, herself a Frenchperson, "You have no respect for food. You have cut zis cheese the wrong way." Naturally, we Americans all laugh. Not seeing the humor, Simone thinks we're amused that a chef could go on strike because diners treated her food with disrespect.

Simone sets the plate of cheese on the long plank table where we eat collectively, like a peasant family, out of doors, on this terrace overlooking a valley in Provence. We're here in this restored medieval village near Avignon after having been Tom Sawyered into helping rebuild old dwellings and to practice our French.

The brie on the plate is puddling, now, and the hide is torn and tattered as if clawed by dogs. Simone resembles those tall gaunt Appalachians in Walker Evans' Depression photos, so her somber gaze is powerfully reproachful as it admonishes us to look at the damage we've done.

She tsks-tsks. There is a correct way to carve the cheese, she says in French. You must learn or Irene won't cook for you.

Well, we know deep down that this has been coming on. Day before yesterday, my wife, Marcia, had been assigned sous chef duties and had overheard Irene muttering to herself that we *"ne savent pas se tenir a table."* Aside from our "disrespect" to the cheese, we also waste bread and eat courses in any order that strikes our prodigal whim!

Irene has a postgraduate degree in French history, which alone would give her an exaggerated estimation of the importance of France to the world, and when you add the congenital jingoism that is her Gallic birthright, and top it off with your chef's usual bombastic touchiness (a universal trait, supposedly), you've got a very volatile individual with considerable power to honk. The French honk like geese to express disgust and contempt, apparently their most commonly experienced emotions, and even though Irene's got a very cute little nose, her nostrils can flare and she can snort a resonating Bb with the best of them.

Like I say, we're all — Yanks and Danes and Finns and Brits and Italians — pretty sure Irene's not in a snit just because of this mangled pie of brie before us. We stand about feeling a little hurt. The comment overheard in her kitchen about our manners has incited some resentment. I admit to some chagrin, too, since Irene is one of many petite French women I've worked up a crush on, a fact known to my wife. (There's something about them — they're so angry all the time, and they're always glowering and chainsmoking and lecturing: they could make your life so miserably interesting!)

Simone sighs sadly, wheels about and returns to the kitchen, leaving the ravaged brie for us to contemplate as if it were a dead kitten tortured by sadistic boys.

"You think Irene's upset about that food fight?" Bob ventures. Bob, a retired ad executive from Pennsylvania, is very, uh, outgoing. He started the food fight last night at supper, but we were all guilty of pitching in, so to speak. It seemed downright festive.

In our defense, it was pretty tame. No cream pies, no pudding, no mashed potatoes. No sticky stuff or liquids. We'd spent the afternoon on a very pleasant excursion tramping through sunny pastures and vineyards for several kilometers to a cherry orchard, where our leader, Ginoux (husband to Simone), passed out pails and we filled them with ripe, succulent cherries. We brought these back to the village, and when they showed up on the supper table with cheese for dessert, we toyed with our food. Truth is, we'd had a few hundred apiece during the picking, and we were a tad bored with eating them.

What's left, then? Somebody challenged somebody else to a mouth-catch (bear in mind that we eat our meals outside at a big plank table on a terrace overlooking a valley in Provence), which soon evolved into a variation you might call mouth-catch doubles where pairs of players tried to toss cherries into their partners' mouths, which inspired a pit-spit, which... well, you can see where this went. Soon you've got a long plank table on a terrace overlooking a valley in Provence where fifteen or so madcap non-Frenchpersons are cutting up like adolescents, flinging cherries and patooee-ing pitwads in one another's hair, and meanwhile the chefs are looking on in *quelle horreur!* from the kitchen and are flapping and honking at one another like they're SOS-ing the flock together to wing out of here South quick as they can.

"Jeez!" says Jerry to Simone's back. He's a retired railroad engineer from Minnesota. "It's not like this is formal dining or anything."

"There's not even napkins," puts in Clark, who hides Kleenex in his pockets when he comes to the table. Whether for political (ecological), economic, or cultural reasons, napkins aren't offered with meals.

When we arrived here about a week ago, we all sat down to this long table made of timbers salvaged from an ancient river barge, sat, as I've said, in the dappled light under an arbor on the terrace overlooking this valley in Provence, and we were properly awed by *l'ambiance*. Meals are served family-style. We each eat from a large white bowl — salad or soup first — then we're expected to wipe the bowl clean with bits of bread and put the ahn-tray and side dishes in it next, clean the bowl again for dessert, etc. Loaves of bread the size of baseball bats are set right upon the bare table (birds roost in the arbor overhead), and we tear off hunks with our hands. Cats wind in and out of our legs, and now and then a dog noses up to beg. Pigeons coo from a nearby stone tower in the waning, elongated summer twilight. Fig trees border the terrace. Down the hill are old stone buildings of the village that date to the Middle Ages. You can hear faint strains of Bach from someone's piano. From where we sit we can smell manure and honeysuckle and fresh bread baking in the ovens of the *boulangerie* down on the village square.

All this was a novelty, for sure. At first we took care to ask our neighbors politely to please pass this and that, then as we grew more familiar with one another and were also afflicted with typical American impatience, the boarding-house reach became the standard method of getting something you wanted, and if somebody down the way does bother to ask you to pass those potatoes please in front of you, you give yourself an extra helping before you send the bowl on, and everyone who's in the relay takes a portion, too. The absence of napkins and waiters, the *al fresco* aspect, the way we bus and wash our own dishes, the fact that at lunch we're eating in our dusty work clothes — these and many other details of how we dine have encouraged a standard of etiquette belitting a drunken fraternity barbeque.

But we're eager to make amends with Irene. It's not just a matter of national pride, either, or a wish to avoid an international incident. We don't want her to go on strike. She's French, remember: we would miss her mayonnaise chicken, her *carottes râpées*, her *salade Niçoise*, her chocolate cakes, her chunky cherry jam (we picked 'em!), her Gallic version of shepherd's pie, her *fromage blanc* with apricots, her lentil salad, her Hungarian eggs, her beef stew, her potato soup (she pushes the potatoes and a local green through a sieve), her quiches, her Provençal paella, her cheesecakes, cheese souffles, her peach and cherry tarts, her cold asparagus salad.

By her own request, Marcia has had sous chef duty more than any of us, and since she overheard Irene cursing about our bad manners, we dispatch her to invite Irene outside onto the terrace so we can apologize and grovel for a second chance.

After a moment, they come out together. Irene's about 5'1"

and weighs maybe 105 pounds. She wears ballet slippers and form-fitting designer jeans and simple cotton blouses sometimes accessorized by a scarf, and if you cross her vapor trail you catch a delicate, understated whiff of very good perfume. She frowns well, too. French women are excellent at frowning.

She speaks no English, not to us at least. While we stand about sheepishly, Marcia explains to Irene that we are embarrassed about our behavior, *certainement*, and hope to be forgiven, but we also beg for her to realize that the very rudimentary fashion of our meal-taking here — *sans serviette, sans* plate for *le pain*, etc. — has encouraged us to believe that we were behaving as French peasants would given the same conditions — *comme on dit, dans la maniéré Française.*

I thought that argument was a brilliant stroke on Marcia's part. Irene, however, honked like a Peterbilt airhorn on a downhill coast.

"*Mais non!* Manners have nothing to do with napkins or utensils!" she declared in her mother tongue. "Even a poor country man with plates and bowls that are all chipped and broken will have respect for the food!" She cocked her hand like a pistol and hip-shot that poor tortured brie.

Marcia purred, "*Bien entendu!* Perhaps Madame le chef would teach us the proper treatment of *cette fromage.*"

Irene did some frowning exercises just as a warm-up, then muttered, "*D'accord.*" She went into the kitchen and returned a moment later with a knife.

She gathered us around the end of the table for the lesson. You take the knife *comme ça*, she said, and you bring it down onto the wedge of brie as if the wedge were a pie, and you cut from the outer rim down to the center the precise size of the piece that you desire, no more or less! Under no circumstances do you do *comme ça!* (She held the knife over the point of the wedge as if to cut across it.) And *jamais jamais jamais* dig into it *comme ça!* (Here, she shuddered as she mimed gouging at the cheese and digging out the soft center from under the hide.) You must take the rind, too! You do not have to eat it — some do, some do not — but never never never *comme ça!* (Once again, shuddering, her eyelids fluttering as if she might faint even to consider such a desecration, she repeated a mime of gouging under the rind.) Suddenly palming the table for support, she added that she once saw an American use a spoon!

We all went *Quelle horreur!* then *merci beaucouped!* her a few dozen times, and while she stood by to supervise, we took turns slicing along the radial axis to take a slender portion so that when you lifted it away, the wedge of brie was the same shape as before but smaller.

Placated, Irene went back on the job, and that night she had Ginoux go down into the village and get a particularly good red from a fellow who made it right in his own cellar, and she gave us her roast pork loin with garlic and rosemary and parsley potatoes. From then on, we kept our figurative elbows off the table, and so everyone was happy.

A Postcard from the Algarve

*My Jeurs secretly walk me to where
they can see themselves*

The weather is toeing the line between winter and spring;
it's the time of year when back home one warm day will
cajole jonquils and peach trees into bloom and the next night's
freeze will bite them for presumption. Here in Tavira on the
Mediterranean coast, the Portuguese locals huddle in heavy
woolen sweaters and caps over their ears while Nordic and
English tourists here for the sun wear shorts of denial.

It rains for three days straight, not steadily, but off and on,
an hour or two in early morning, with a crisp stiff wind rushing in off the ocean and tug-boating huge cloud crafts ahead of
it so gray and flat-bottomed big that to look up at that wheeling
mass makes you dizzy. After noon, the ceiling breaks apart and
the sun starts poking through by fits and starts, for moments
at a time, and everybody's mood lifts a little. So on the afternoon of this third day I go out to run a few errands in the brief
sunbreak between the rainy chill of morning and the cold of
darkness.

We've been gone from home three weeks to the day.
Because of the usual Byzantine rules of ticket purchasing, it

was cheaper to buy excursion-fare round-trip tickets and use only the departure half than to buy a one-way ticket. We've kept up a running joke for twenty days about how if we really don't want to commit to this trip for six months we can always go back on that return ticket on the 21st day.

This morning, we both did a countdown with our watches as the return flight to our home in America lifted off from Madrid at 9:07 without us. We were both swept by a wave of homesickness and had to gulp back our fear.

As a result, my parents, and my children — off to college and barely out of adolescence, it seems — are on my worried mind. When you give anxiety free rein to create nightmarish scenarios, then the distance from those you love seems oddly to lessen their hold on life, as if your presence itself were a useful device to them for keeping that grip.

Feeling skittish and off-center, I go out hoping to snare a bit of the fitful sunshine and to convince myself I want to be a tourist nonstop for six months and to be away from my family. I shop in the market for bread and fruit and, since the sun looks as if it might hold up for a while, I decide to walk *Rue Tenente Couto* up the hill to the old Sao Francisco monastery, which I've meant to see for days. Far in the distance to the south, blue sheets of rain hang from clouds over the Mediterranean. Above my head, the gray scud glides by, but it has frazzled into tatters and faded to the color of coal steam, so it doesn't look too threatening.

The Sao Franciso monastery is not in use as such, but guidebooks praise the garden just off the street. Now it's empty but for a workman in overalls slowly spading a diamond of moist dark earth near the back wall. A network of gravel

paths symmetrically dissects the garden to leave mosaics of
planted soil between; if you saw it from overhead, you might
think of the ceiling in a Romanesque church. Some diamonds
contain grass cut tee-off close which the recent rains have
greened up to the hue of clover; in others there are bushes from
which single yellow roses the size of Texas grapefruits droop
and sway on the ends of thorny stalks too slender to support
them. Palm trees, kalanchoe, gallardias, a very familiar prickly-
pear — it seems odd to me that this garden has so many plants
native to my own region of the planet. I toy with the idea that
a mysterious homing principle has led me here: my nostrils detected the familiar pollen, say, and sent a message to my brain
that my conscious mind did not know how to read, and my
brain whispered *home* to my feet too low for me to hear.

I stroll the gravel walks mortaring the diamond-shaped
plots a while, letting my market bag bump my knee and sniff-
ing the ozoned air for the faint but detectable cologne of those
roses. I fight off the compulsion to trace the territory's formal
grid in a systematic fashion and instead try bee-like to let my
eye lead me from one flower to another.

The workman ignores me, keeps up his ruminant's rhythm
with the shovel. We've done a kind of dance, really: when I
came in off the street, I was aware that he stood square near
the back guarding this space, and I stepped into it like a stray
cat, as if the emptiness alone were cause for caution. As I've
made it more my own, forging deeper, feeling more familiar,
the workman has followed his own compulsive row-work and
has spaded himself to the front of the garden near the street.
Now instead of protecting the garden from my intrusion he's
trapped me in it and drives me into deeper exploration.

At the back of the garden runs a wall of stone some ten feet tall. I walk along it until I reach a break. There's a rusted wrought-iron gate; it has fallen back from its latch, leaving a gap of several inches a child could slip through.

Through the gate's rusting bars you can see an abandoned courtyard? Another garden? A secret garden? Well, another large plot surrounded by thick stone walls, at any rate, about the size of the formal garden I've just strolled through. The plot is shagged with tall weeds and uncut grass, clumps of unruly shrubs and unpruned fruit trees. The fallow greenery has snagged old crumpled papers, wrappers and refuse — I see a few rusted paint cans lying half-hidden on their flanks, butt ends of rotting lumber.

The rear wall draws my eye. Embedded in the thick stone flank are bins, a honeycomb of bins, which gives the wall the appearance of a wasp's nest from this distance. Some bins are open and empty, others have yawning doors, while others still sealed off bear rectangular plates. Name plates? Were the ashes of monks stored there in that wall and later moved elsewhere?

I look back toward the street. The workman's spade stands jabbed upright in a mound of soil, but he has vanished. The garden is still deserted. Except for the huge cloud shadows that lumber over these walls like silent, invisible aircraft, I'm alone. I squeeze myself through the gap in the rusting gate, get a streak the color of dried blood across my chest for my trouble.

I step to the side of the gate so I can't be seen from the street. I don't know why I should feel so furtive, but I do. And it's not as if I want to hide from any authority — it's a little as if I don't want this deserted place to register my presence, don't want my presence to make it any less deserted: it's like standing in the forest and trying to be invisible while watching the tree fall so that you'll know at last if it can be heard if no one's there.

Centered in the plot is a lemon tree; the lemons high in its branches have turned yellow, those on the lower boughs are still green as the leaves. Next to the tree stands an odd piece of sculpture? It's as tall as a man — there's a base of marble half-obscured by tall grass, then four columns come up from the corners to support a marble canopy. Under the canopy there's a slender human figure standing with its back to the gate; the figure is draped Grecian-style, the toga slipped from one thin shoulder to show the nude back, a delicate spine and nape, narrow hips, the figure of a woman?

No, a child.

The marble child peers toward the honeycombed wall. One elbow rests upon the lip of an urn and the child's cheek is charmingly laid upon that palm, the posture sad? pensive? melancholy? and at the base of the figure words are carved into the stone.

The shattered overcast shoves a window open; I hold my breath as sunbeams do a crazy goose-step across the yard then march away and leave me shivering in the chill. Now I know what sort of place I'm in. I see the other signs, headstones poking above the rubble. The wind gusts up, shakes a flurry of white blossoms out of an almond tree, and they swirl about; they snow all over us, me and the marble child, somebody's child who plays alone over his own bones in this neglected graveyard.

The Kindness of Strangers

Considering the necessity and danger of trust

As the bus wheeled out of the loading bay, the girl stepped
in front of it and stiff-armed her hand like a cop, and the driver,
eyes rolling, hit the brakes. We were still half-inside the Lisbon
station, and by my watch we were already seven minutes late.
The driver cranked the front door open, but the girl stood her
ground and pointed, neither obstinately nor apologetically, to
the enormous pack that rode above her shoulders like a piggy-
backed child. The driver had to dismount and step off to open
the belly of the bus so she could stow it.

She passed our seats going to the rear. She was maybe five-
two or so, baggy blue sweater and jeans, sandy hair in a pony-
tail, no makeup on a face plain as a vanilla wafer. I thought she
might be American, English, Australian, or Canadian, maybe
even German. But we three were the only apparent foreigners
on this bus in late January bound for Evora, a small hill town
in the interior of Portugal, and that this small, young female
was traveling alone seemed exceptional. She made me think
(worry about?) my 20-year-old daughter.

At the station in Evora, Marcia went off to find the restrooms while I sat in the waiting room and used the compass on my watch to orient myself on the map of Evora in my green Michelin guide. When I looked up, the girl was sitting out-of-harness nearby and was reading a very familiar guide book with a red cover. Since we consulted the same book with the frequency and regularity of Muslims at prayer, the girl suddenly became a familiar category to me.

"I see you're a *Let's Go* traveler, too."

"Yeah," she said. "I was wondering about the youth hostel, where it is from here."

Her accent was American. I looked up the address, checked it against my Michelin green, ostentatiously flashed the compass on my watch, showed her where we were on the map, which way to walk from the station, how far to go. I fairly beat her over the head with my organizational and orienteering skills — I mean, I could've easily told her how to get there without showing off how I came by the information. It's a kind of sickness in us both that we take such insufferable pride in our powers of preparedness and work so hard to ward off the unexpected, the unpredictable, the boogey-man who lurks in wait for those who rely on luck or the kindness of strangers. And, okay, yeah, sometimes it means extra work — twice recently I'd gone to buy train tickets to some place only to learn that you can't buy tickets until the day you travel, the idea of which makes persons like me collapse into quivering heebie-jeebies.

Giving her more directions than she needed, I knew that something insidiously paternal was at work in me; I think I wanted to give her a lesson in how she must behave if she was to ward off the hazards of traveling alone as a woman, as if I had more experience at it. With an L.L. Bean compass-watch and a good map, she wouldn't have to rely on a strange man in a bus station.

She said, "You know if this station has lockers? I'd like to store my pack while I go look for a place."

"No, I don't. I'd be glad to watch your gear if you want to check, though."

She hesitated only slightly then rose and said, "Thanks."

"I'm just waiting for my wife — she's in the restroom," I said, even though she had already given me dominion over her belongings.

She went off empty-handed. I slid her pack and its attached sleeping bag closer to our two bags. I was curious to know what all she was carrying. It seemed a wonder to me that this child would wander Europe alone with no more provisions than the pack, the book, some money, though that was precisely our case, too. I saw her parents at home biting their nails. It wouldn't be long before my daughter would be graduating college and might even expect to be allowed to do this same thing, though in truth "allow" is not a relevant verb in regard to a college graduate unless she's still on the dole.

The young woman had trusted me with everything. She carried no purse, so I guessed her passport and money were tucked inside, though a travel wallet might be hidden on her person. I was glad she had someone as trustworthy as me to watch her bags; I felt a little like the driver who picks up a young hitchhiker expressly to protect her from predators and to lecture her on the dangers of hitchhiking.

When Marcia appeared at my elbow, I said, "I'm watching that American girl's backpack."

I passed the baton to her and went off to find "Senhors."

When I came back, Marcia was still there but the pack was gone.

"Where'd she go?"

"She hoofed it to the hostel." Marcia said that her name was Barbara and she was from Chicago; she was 23, the youngest of three children. She'd given up a job in the graphics department of a textbook publisher to spend nine months traveling, and her parents didn't understand why she had to do it. Her father is worried about her future because her older siblings are married and have respectable careers. Her periods last for twelve hours and she's on the Pill.

"She told you all that?"

"She could tell I was the big sister type. Maybe she's a little lonely. I told her where we're going to stay and invited her to come have dinner."

We checked into our hostel, had drinks on the too-chilly terrace in pale January sunshine, and unpacked at a leisurely pace, but by forty-five minutes past the meeting time, Barbara from Chicago hadn't shown. This didn't surprise me, so we went out without her. When we returned, the desk clerk gave us a note: "Sorry to miss dinner. Got lost. Maybe later? Barbara from Chicago."

We had no idea when "later" meant. The picture of a lonely child wandering the streets of a foreign city in search of someone as remotely familiar as us inspired my pity, but I could lay the blame in getting lost to insufficient attention to one's surroundings. Feeling sorry for young people suffering the consequences of their mistakes is a familiar emotion to any parent with teenagers, and I was hardened to it.

"Later" turned out to be three weeks. We'd gone on to the

Algarve, to Seville and to Cordoba, and had just stepped off
the train in Ronda, Spain, when I thought I spotted her. She
was fully loaded and was walking along the platform away
from us, so I couldn't be sure.

"Hey, Chicago!" I yelled.

"She's got earbuds in," said Marcia.

I hung back with our bags on my shoulders while Marcia,
who could as easily have been a purse-snatcher as an acquaintance, chased after her and came up from behind to flag her
down. Then we all sat in the station snackbar like longtime
friends drinking Coke Light (them) and a Mahou, a Spanish
beer (me). After missing us in Evora, she'd gone to Lagos and
to that windswept southwesternmost point of the Continent,
Sagres, then back to Lisbon and Madrid before coming down
here.

It seems peculiar, now, how eagerly we remet and shared
our recent adventures given that we'd only known her for a few
minutes back in Evora. I'd come to take for granted this kind
of remarkable coincidence of coming across a fellow traveler
unexpectedly in another city, as it had already happened to
us more than once: the couple you murmured good morning
to in the dining room of your hostel in Avignon, France, will
possibly show up in the dining room of your hostel in Assisi,
Italy, partly because you're using the same guide book and no
one on a European tour will visit an ugly place.

Already on the road we'd made over a dozen 24-hour pals
in different cities. Diane and Jim in Madrid, Polly and Joe and
Patrick in Lisbon, Barbara Chicago in Evora and now Ronda,
Erik and Kelly in Cordoba, Brian and Jill in Seville, Kevin and
Sue and Robert and Eva in Tavira, Portugal — Americans,

Aussies, Danes. Trust-fund hippies, retired nurses, under-
grads, engineers and accountants and chemists on leave. It was
a little breathtaking and yet vaguely unsettling how I'd find
myself feeling the bonds of The Brotherhood of the Backpack.
Within minutes strangers whose surnames I rarely learned
could come to seem like friends of long standing solely on the
basis that we had in common this wholly absorbing undertak-
ing we'd set aside our normal lives to pursue. The need for support and comfort, the need to talk about what has happened,
the need to trade notes, to find relief from the unrelenting
foreignness — these too partly drove us all together. That we
all had to do this on the cheap also lent an air of politically
correct snobbery to the enterprise.

Others in the Brotherhood were truly innocent of character defects before proven guilty. We trusted them implicity.
The posture we seemed to strike toward them was to be wholly
open and receptive, willing to grant the benefit of the doubt,
willing even to lend money or to borrow it without discomfort:
Patrick, a student from California, went with us to hear *fado* in
Lisbon and when the bill caught me off-guard, he put up thirty
bucks on our behalf without blinking.

Yet about all our quick new pals we knew almost nothing
substantial. What little we did know came from their mouths
only. It seemed to me, though, that because they'd put themselves on this road I could automatically deposit into his or
her account a starter fund of intelligence, curiosity, hardiness,
generosity, and liberality only because it was hard to imagine
a depressive, paranoiac tightwad with a yen to swindle putting him or herself into these traces. It was possible that these
pals we met might actually possess these virtues and vices, but

down deep I knew that my estimate of them didn't derive from any close scrutiny of their behavior.

Barbara Chicago decided to take *Let's Go's* first recommendation for accommodations in Ronda. While her choice had no heat, she usually cocooned in her sleeping bag, anyway, and the place had a terrace looking down into El Tajo, the gorge the town roosted over. We chose another hostel that cost a little more but might be — albeit temporarily or intermittently or even only rarely — heated. We made plans to meet her in front of Turismo at 7 for dinner.

We showed up five minutes early, which for us is five minutes late. I wasn't expecting Barbara Chicago to be on time, but she wasn't very tardy. At 7:15 she strolled up accompanied by a young man. I almost failed to recognize her. She was wearing a red blazer-like garment with gold-spangled epaulets and gold braid festooning the sleeves and cuffs — it reminded me of the Curious George books or a ringmaster's coat. Her pink lipstick clashed against that cherry blazer, but it did liven up her face, as did the dated blue eyeshadow on her upper lids. Long loopy silver earrings, her hair combed out around her shoulders. She looked pretty fetching, actually. She looked like a woman ready for a night on the town. Now she didn't look even remotely like someone who lived out of a backpack.

She'd bought the jacket today in a flea market, she said when Marcia admired it. It seemed a very impractical purchase to me, considering that she'd have to tote it in her backpack, but I admired the impulse and looking at this festive rag cheered us all up.

She introduced the young man as "Antonio, my amigo." With dark hair and black, plastic-rimmed glasses, he bore a vague resemblance to a young Steve Allen, if Steve Allen had had Spanish parents, say. Or Elvis Costello, maybe. He was wearing sneakers, jeans, and a very peculiar sweater — a heavy lemon-yellow turtleneck with zippers that went from his wrists to his jugulars. Under his arm he was carrying a thin but very large manila envelope.

"He knows a good pizza restaurant," said Barbara. "Okay if he joins us?"

"*Su amigo es mi amigo,*" said I, and off we went, even though "good pizza" in Spain was, to me, an oxymoron.

I presumed from the introduction that they knew each other from another time or place, maybe, and were now out on a date, but when we struck out for the restaurant with the ladies behind and the gentlemen leading, he told me they'd just met in the plaza down the way where a British television crew was filming a Honda commercial. Antonio told me he lived in a village about ten kilometers from Ronda and was a student. He seemed too old for that: later at dinner, when Barbara mentioned that she was twenty-three, Antonio said, "I'm twenty-five now." I would've guessed thirty. I don't know why I didn't believe him. Maybe it seemed too low a number for his face and also it seemed to form a suspiciously serendipitous gap, yet likewise a link, between their ages. It allowed him to be a superior peer. I wondered whether he'd have said "28" if she'd said "27."

"I'm studying English all the time," he said.

"You speak it very well." He made a few boners in inflection (he knew an American woman from "o-MAH-ha") and an occasional vocabulary gap left him momentarily marking

time, but he certainly spoke better English than any of us spoke
Spanish, though I couldn't resist practicing mine on him.

The pizzeria had candles and sets of wine glasses stem up
on the tables and napkins perched like party hats on all the
plates. It was exceedingly empty but for a squad of idle waiters lounging near the front door who greeted us exuberantly.
Antonio hailed each by name. I wondered if he got a kick-back.

"I'm vegetarian," Barbara announced while we three
Americans were all looking at our menus. "I don't eat anything
fried in animal fat, either."

"That's pretty hard to do in Portugal and Spain," said
Marcia. I too was thinking of how a Hindu traveling in West
Texas might be hard put finding something to eat at the Dairy
Queens.

"Especially if you don't speak the languages," Barbara added with a grin. "Usually I eat stuff out of grocery stores or markets or I walk around in a cafe with a waiter in tow and point
to other people's plates."

With Antonio's aid, Barbara ordered an omelet with cheese
and boiled potatoes — to judge by the three trips made to the
kitchen by our waiter, this last was an eccentric request. We
took the everything-pizza advertised as the house specialty.
Antonio ordered only coffee.

"You're not eating?" I asked.

"I'll eat later. With my family."

"With your wife and children?" I asked devilishly.

"Not me!" he crowed. "Not me! No, not me!" He gave
Barbara a sidelong glance.

"I thought every Spanish man had a wife and a mistress."

"You got to have money to be married."

"Antonio, if you're hungry, please eat," Marcia told him. "We'd be pleased to make it our treat since you were so helpful in bringing us here."

"Thank you. It is too early for me."

It was about 8:30. The Spanish dinner hour was around ten, which might explain why the restaurant was empty.

"Well," said Barbara. "This is sure a beautiful town. Antonio, you're lucky to live here."

He shrugged. "It's boring. There's no work. From May to September, I go to Barcelona and work in a restaurant up there." He reached under his chair and brought up the manila envelope and rattled it. "Eck-us rays. The government gives me money now. My knee." He made a slashing motion with the edge of his hand. "Futbol."

"You were on a team?"

"No. Just some chicos." He grinned. "But I was making the big score."

The pizza was, as expected, an odd concoction featuring a base of cheese topped by pale tomato slices swimming in olive oil and a fried egg sunnyside up in the center.

"Very good," I told Antonio. It was what an Englishman looking for breakfast in Italy might have dreamed up, given the addition of a banger or two.

Antonio went off to make a phone call, he said. Though I already knew the answer, I asked Barbara if she'd known Antonio long.

She laughed. "Like two hours."

"Do you get hit on a lot traveling alone?" asked Marcia.

She shrugged. "There are jerks everywhere in the world. I get hassled in Chicago, too."

"Don't you ever feel at risk?"

"Yeah, sure. But no more or less than I do at home on a regular day if I have to go downtown and walk by a construction site."

"Have you had any close calls here?" Marcia asked.

"Well, I dunno really. I guess I've been pretty lucky considering some of the things I've done."

"What've you done?"

Barbara held back a second or two, then she said, "Well, like last week, when I went to Sagres. I met this guy on the train from Sweden. He was really pretty good looking, you know, and he was a little younger than me and he spoke kind of student English with this real cute accent. We fell in together when we got there. It's off-season, you know, so there's not much going on. We went out and walked along the famous cliffs and looked at the ocean, but it was really windy and very cold. Anyway, we went to dinner at a really nice place. I don't know what got into me, I mean I don't usually do this, but I drank a whole bottle of wine by myself, and I got really drunk."

She paused as if this was where the story ended, and I thought it would be indelicate to prompt for more, but she went on without it.

"So I woke up the next morning in this strange room." Her eyes were closed but she was smiling from one corner of her mouth as though at her own stupidity but wasn't sure she should be. "I kind of blacked out. I've only done that a couple times before, you know, way back in high school. Anyway, the guy was gone. All the stuff in my backpack was dumped out on the floor."

"Wow! Was anything missing?"

"He didn't take any money. I got pretty panicky when I couldn't find my passport, but after a while I realized I was in a hostel and I finally figured out that one of us had probably given it to the desk clerk the night before."

"What was he looking for, then, drugs?"

"I don't know. I'm pretty sure he did take some panties."

Her laughing at herself invited us to join in, so I did, but I was appalled.

"Weren't you horrified?" asked Marcia.

"Well, at the time I think I was more mad that he'd stuck me with the bill."

My theory: Barbara Chicago had a happy childhood. I can think of no innocence more profound than that of a young person who has had competent, loving parents. Such a child comes to trust that "everything will work out" or that it's best "not to worry." Such a child puts his or her trust in others, or in "fate" or "luck" or relies on "instinct" to deliver what he or she needs, never realizing that the projections into the future are based on a (short) lifetime of having had their "luck" created and augmented, solidified and honed by dutiful and loving parents.

Barbara Chicago was the youngest of three children and so she had the advantage of being parented by five persons, and this bountiful parenting may have formed a kind of bell jar, and inside it she's always safe. Being a parent, realizing that so much of her "luck" comes from efforts of others, I shuddered to imagine that she imagined that she's "pretty lucky."

We're all vulnerable here. We trust other travelers because the capacity for trust is the traveler's salient virtue, whether by temperament or just the sheer necessary exercise of it, and his or her most useful tool.

We have little choice but to trust in the kindness of strangers. Most are foreigners on whom we have an almost child-like dependency because we rely on them for basic necessities I recall how in a market in Jaipur, India, I wanted to buy an orange. I felt like a two-year-old. Lacking the word for it, I had to pick it up in one hand, and, because I couldn't even ask "how much" or if I had I wouldn't have understood the stall-keeper's reply, I masked my face with a moronic smile of what I hoped was ingratiating helplessness, then I held out a palm full of rupees. Nodding toward my hand like an idiot, I invited the seller to take the correct coins for the orange or to cheat me with the relish of the oppressed encountering a sudden run of luck. The choice was hers. I felt at once foolish yet saintly, as if I had chosen to put this woman in an exalted state of trust, and, in doing so, I was secretly hoping that such virtuous behavior couldn't inspire anything less than a corresponding honesty and admiration. I made a virtue of necessity.

We have to trust our guide books or throw them away. Should I trust the tap water? (We did, in Europe at least, without harm.) Should I trust the cab driver to get me to a place I've never seen or been before from a place I've never been or seen before? This clean cut young man who saunters up while I'm peering at my map on a busy street corner and who offers to help — is he a friendly native who likes being an ambassador or does he lead a gang of cutthroats?

The bank tellers who change my money — should I trust

them or count the bills myself? (That's easily done. My report
on this particular issue is that a Lisbon teller in pre-euro days
tried to give me 167,000 *escudos* rather than the 176,000 that
were due me, but a currency-exchange clerk in Nice made a
$170 mistake in francs in my favor. We argued with him for a
full five minutes before he understood, and when at last he did,
he was passionately grateful.)

I have to trust the concierge not to lose my passport or to
sell it on the black market while I sleep. I have to trust ticket
agents know their business, though in at least two cases we
got tickets that bore the wrong dates or seats that had already
been consigned to other persons. Such mistakes often happen
in our own country, certainly, but we don't usually have to sit
on a suitcase while they're being fixed or attempt to straighten
them out by using a language we only began to speak the day
before yesterday. At home you know the avenues of recourse
for bungled bills and shoddy work and outright skullduggery.

As for trusting your "instincts" — it turns out that what
we thought were our "instincts" about other people or a situation were feelings that depended upon an elaborate system of coded signals derived purely from a cultural context.
We could no longer judge with certainty whether we'd been
complimented or insulted by a phrase or a gesture, and, not
knowing, we couldn't trust our own responses. Accustomed
to being wary of people who approach you on the streets of
Anywhere in America, you ignore the Senhora of a hostel who
has come to the bus station in a small Portuguese town to find
guests for her perfectly spotless and charming home (an ad in
the Yellow Pages here would be ludicrously inefficient), and be-

cause you shun her you wind up where you deserve to be: in a filthy, overpriced hotel catering solely to tourist groups.

But, oh, the horror stories we tell around our campfires! Erik and Cindy went to Tangiers, took care to ignore the hundreds of hawkers and pestiferous "guides" at the landing, but eventually when they were ready to return, they got lost and had to stop and ask someone how to reach the bus station. The fellow they asked guided them through a spooky medina and deep into an empty cul-de-sac where he started shouting and demanding that they pay him $50. "I didn't know what to do," said Erik. "I mean, if somebody did that to me in the States and he didn't have a weapon, I'd just say, 'Fuck off!' But we didn't have any idea where we were or who lived around there. We were lost. I offered him $10 and he took it, then he told us how to get to the bus station."

Molly had her purse snatched in Sicily by boys on a motorcycle. Eric and Joe set their backpacks down in a bar, and while they had a couple of beers, somebody made off with one of them. Late one night, Jim and Lynn let a taxi driver take them from the train station in Athens to some distant, squalid suburb; he dropped them off at a house where seven men were staying, one of whom offered to rent them an adjoining doorless, dirt-floor shed for the night. They told him they'd take it, and, when his back was turned, they heaved their bags through a window, climbed out after them, and made their way back to the city, chased through the dark, unpaved streets by loose dogs and lively shadows.

The trick is not to be paralyzed by suspicion; the most prudent course is also going to be the dullest. That which carries no risk also yields no adventure or pleasure. You could say the safest thing to do is to stay at home, except that in our old neighborhood, we often heard gunshots on weekend nights, every house on the block had been burgled at least once, the street outside our window was often sprinkled with sparkling window shards where thieves whisked away somebody's car during the night, and in the first week after we left for Europe a fellow walking through at 8 p.m. was robbed and stabbed. Familiarity alone gives you a false sense of security, and you forget that almost any American city has more murders in it per year than all of the nations of Western Europe combined. Hearing of an terrorist bombing in London, people change their travel plans by visiting their agent on a street where passersby are routinely mugged and often stabbed or shot.

When we left the restaurant, locals were drifting in to take their supper, and Spanish nightlife was dawning. But Marcia and I were weary. This had been a moving-base-camp day, and we were anxious to end it. We all stood uncertainly for a moment in a plaza where a squadron of mopeds was mercilessly strafing pedestrians.

Antonio shouted over them. "I am going to a bar owned by a friend of mine, where students go! Would you like to go with me?" He addressed us all, but his gaze, hungry and plaintive, landed last on Barbara.

"I think we'll turn in," I said.

"Me, too," said Barbara.

I wondered if this was for our benefit or to let Antonio know she was getting off the "date." I wondered if we should offer to walk her to her hostel, but I didn't want to risk offending Antonio by implying she needed protection. Or offending her. She'd been traveling in Europe for three months without any such "protection."

Marcia, wondering the same, said, "Will you be ok?"

"Oh, sure."

"Do you know where you are?" I asked.

"I will show you how to get there," said Antonio.

We all walked back toward the center of town for a few blocks, then came to a crossroad where according to Antonio's gestures we would go right and Barbara to the left.

"This way," he said to her. "My friend's bar is this way, too."

I looked at Barbara to make certain she wasn't sending us any last-second pleas for help, but she gave us an adios wave as the two of them stepped off away from us.

"You think she'll be ok?" I asked after they'd vanished into a crowd of milling young people across the plaza.

"Hope so."

The next day, we were sitting sunning our faces in the park that overlooks the gorge when Antonio walked up and hailed us. At least, I thought, he hadn't fled after murdering our Chicago pal. We chatted with him a bit, and he seemed to be looking about distractedly. He was wearing that same yellow sweater with the zippers, but I could smell cologne.

"We went to the gorge this morning. *Muy linda!*"

He smirked. He laid his cheek against his hands.

"You slept late."

"Yeah. But my mother keeps waking me, shaking me, she

thinks I'm dead or something, and she wants me to eat."

When we lapsed into silence, the suspense got to him. "Where's Barbara?"

"I'm not sure," I said. "You saw her last."

He grinned wolfishly. "She is a nice girl. I like American girls. I like Japanese and Danish girls, too."

Maybe it was the addition of "Danish," but he sounded like a gourmet.

"You don't like Spanish women?"

He did that Continental "puh!" with lips and breath that expresses contempt. "They don't care about anything but getting husbands."

This was in contrast to, he said, foreign women he'd known. Like the girl from o-MAH-ha. Also, he'd known one from Portland, Oregon. She came to Spain with her husband and they were going to spend three months traveling. They came to the cafe in Barcelona where Antonio was working. They were looking for someone to show them around town. When he went to where he was supposed to meet them, she was alone.

"We had a love affair for those whole three months. We had an apartment. Her husband went off by himself. She still writes to me. I have letters —" he measured a stack in the air between his hands about a foot high.

Then there was a Japanese girl who'd come to Ronda to study Spanish. "She lived where Barbara is staying. Actually, I know every room there very well." He closed his eyes and gave a nostalgic sigh as if suddenly awash in a wave of memories. I think we both wanted to burst into laughter at him but were fairly certain we weren't supposed to. "The Señora is very sympathetic," he added, and I waited to see if he would wink as if to suggest that her "sympathy" went beyond collusion with his amorous plans, but no, he merely meant that the proprietress of the hostel most recommended by *Let's Go* for its view of the gorge willingly looks the other way when a local comes to court a guest in her rented room, of which Barbara is the latest. So much for security.

After her course of study, the Japanese girl moved on to Malaga.

"It was terrible!" Antonio gasped, gnashing his teeth. "I went there every day on the bus, two hours there and back. I could not sleep! I could not eat!" He wrung his hands. He might any moment burst into grief-stricken sobs. "She was the first I truly loved."

"Aw," clucked Marcia.

"So I like Japanese girls," he concluded cheerfully.

The "so" suggested a connection of logic, of deduction, but how he jumped from one beloved Japanese female to a nation of them was beyond me. Was he saying he was doomed to search forever in all female Oriental faces for the visage of the lost loved one?

"She married this Italian guy and now she lives in Padua. She still writes letters to me." Again, the gesture that measured the stack, though apparently this lost lover lacked the Portland woman's zeal for correspondence.

As for the Danish girl: she was with a group of foreigners in a cafe and he and some friends introduced themselves. During the conversation Antonio discovered that the following day was the Danish girl's birthday and that the group was going down to the bottom of the gorge for a picnic. The next morning he went to a girlfriend's house and asked her to make a birthday cake. He then borrowed another friend's bicycle and rode over the bridge and up the street to the head of the path leading into the gorge... Here Antonio paused to act out the dangers of the bike trip with the cake, one hand splayed in the air like a waiter with a loaded tray, the traffic whizzing by (*phew! phew! phew!*), the chuck holes, near-misses, the cake wobbling, almost tumbling, etc. Then, he said, he hiked to the bottom of the gorge, spotted the party in a field, had to climb under a fence (more choreography), then over a wall, and so forth (he was making it clear that the subject of the tale was his efforts), and, at last, into the picnicking circle he comes with the cake, which he presents to the beautiful Danish girl....

"And she was so happy! And grateful!" He gave me a wink.

"I would think so!" said Marcia. "How romantic of you!"

"I did it for three other girls, too."

Maybe he thought this quadrupled the power the story would have on us, but instead he cut it by four.

"Did the same girlfriend make all the cakes?" I asked.

This went right past him, and it was just as well. With the woman from Portland, I'd been interested, and with the Japanese lover I'd been amused, but with the tale of the Dane I'd become aware of myself as an audience. Such bald-faced bragging about one's prowess as a lover — why bother to regale a middle-aged American couple with such stuff? It was harmless enough, of course, but a little pitiful, too. We were safe with the knowledge, I guess. We couldn't test it against any reality.

Maybe he thought Marcia would enjoy hearing of such

attentions being paid in courtship (and presumably imagine herself the vicarious recipient), and in this richly romantic setting to boot: the lovers, poised to say *adios* on the brink of the precipice under the moon the night before she moves on to Malaga, behind them ruins of Moorish castles, gypsy guitar music. Carmen, Carmen, Carmen.

Maybe he wanted to impress me as a male, to make me envious, to make love to my wife right under my nose. It wasn't hard to imagine how these tales might be told differently if we were separately the audience. With only me as the listener, the fabliaux of the married woman from Portland would loom much larger and he'd embellish the story with much more intimate and lusty detail. We'd smoke, spit sunflower seeds while he sketched her parts in the air; winking, we'd adjust our genitals in consideration of this most unvirtuous wife. Then, telling Marcia alone of his grief and his loss of his first love, the Japanese girl, he'd look cow-like into her eyes, seeking pity, admiration.

We're not too many miles from Seville, after all, the birthplace of *Don Juan de Tenorio*, the original story from which all the successive adaptations and derivations were grown. Andalusia, the region, is the home of *Don Juanismo*. Antonio's antics are the Andalusian equivalent to an indigenous crop; he's like cowboys in Texas and surfers in California and lumberjacks in Oregon. Just as Iowa towns have annual festivals celebrating the corn harvest, maybe here in Ronda acting out these old tired roles is like a historical pageant of sorts.

But was Antonio an example from which the cliche is wrought, or had he just worked himself into this weary old routine? Or was he playing to our expectations, just as when Easterners visit us in Dallas, we start saying "yew all" and dust off cowboy boots we haven't worn in years?

What I really thought was that Antonio liked foreign women because his own foreignness was all he had to offer them. Maybe Spanish women took one look and saw an un-employed waiter with no apparent ambition or prospects who at age 30 or so still lived at home with a mother so doting she awakened him from a 12-hour sleep for no reason other than to make sure he ate.

Barbara relieved us by showing up early in the evening and inviting us to a café for *churros* and chocolate. He said Antonio had recommended it, *por supuesto*. It was near the terraced park where we'd seen him earlier that morning and to my surprise had nothing of the air of a spot habituated by local students but instead was obviously the most popular tourist watering hole. We took a metal table on the terrace under strings of naked electric bulbs surrounded by Germans who were still in hiking shorts even though the sun had dropped over the sawtoothed ridges to the West and the air had gone thin and chilled.

Barbara had brought a sketchbook-scrapbook along be-cause she'd been working on it in the park, and she reluctant-ly showed us sketches she'd been doing. The book was made thick and unwieldy by the addition of bar napkins and coast-ers and tickets and little found objects that she'd affixed to the appropriate pages using tape and glue she carried with her. (I wondered what her pack weighed.)

She was showing some sketches of Lisbon (they weren't

bad) when Antonio showed up, greeted us, and took a seat. She'd not leafed another page or two through her book before he started up.

"*Chica!* You have *duende!* The soul of an artiste!"

"Thanks."

"Some day I will be saying I knew her now."

"Surely you and she will still be writing one another," I said.

"It is possible," he said gravely, then turned mournful brown eyes on Barbara. "*Verdad?*"

"Sure," she said lightly enough to shake off all innuendo.

He bent toward her sketchbook and she pulled back slightly and flushed, as if it contained a bare-butt baby picture of her, then when he glanced away she shut the cover.

"I have a friend here, he has a gallery. You should let me take this to him."

She laughed and pulled the book off the table and into her lap. "It's just for me. For my memories."

"I hope you have happy memories of Ronda."

She shrugged. "So far, so good."

"I like your earrings."

"Thanks."

She did send us a look then; she was uncomfortable to be the recipient of such unrelenting and exclusive attention and a little helpless to stop it.

"Do you like mine?" asked Marcia.

"Oh *si!*" cooed Antonio, suddenly coming to himself. "Is it not clear —" this he addressed to me — "that we are with the most beautiful women here?"

"*Sin duda,*" said I. The competition for the honor within

our line of sight all weighed a good fifteen stone, could have most likely heaved a stein all the way across this canyon, and were wearing funny hats.

"Antonio, is there such a thing to you as a woman who is not beautiful?" asked Barbara.

"Truly, no. You can find some beauty in every woman."

"Is her beauty ever irrelevant?" asked Marcia.

Boy, this guy didn't know what he was about to step into.

"Sometimes it is spiritual. An inner beauty." Either he failed to understand the question or was trying to sidestep it.

"I meant is there anything to a woman for you besides this beauty you so dutifully unearth?"

He looked confused. I felt sorry for him.

"Is a woman ever a friend?" put in Barbara.

"Of course!" He sounded indignant.

"Don't you guys remember the one who baked all the cakes?" I said.

"Some are friends. Some are like sisters, some like mothers."

A friend of Antonio's stopped by the table and spoke to him in excellent English, and we were all introduced, and he welcomed us to Ronda. When he left, Barbara said that she wanted to go buy stamps at a *tabac* before it closed.

Antonio rose with her. "I'll show you where it is," he said.

"I know where one is," she said. "But you're welcome to come along anyway."

They left the cafe in tandem with Antonio striking a culturally-minted posture of Spanish males: hands clasped behind his back, torso bent forward slightly, head cocked toward Barbara while talking and listening. Ahead was a flower-vendor's stand. He looked up.

"I bet he buys her a flower," I said.

"How cute!"

They drew closer. He looked from the clumps of carnations to Barbara, who hadn't yet noticed them. If she saw them, he'd have to buy her one. He'd think she expected it. He started talking to her — diverting her attention? Or asking if she'd like a flower? They slowed down, hesitated, but only to hover at the curb.

The moment passed. They stepped off the curb and into the backwash of hurtling mopeds chasing pedestrians down the street.

"Maybe he's too cheap," she said. "Or poor."

"I doubt she'd be too disappointed. Surely she doesn't take that Latin lover stuff seriously."

"Well, you don't have to take it seriously to enjoy it on some level."

"Even if you know it's phony?"

"Well, yes, in a way. I mean you're never sure, just like if somebody praises you for something you do, you don't know if the compliment is genuine or just expedient, right? And you can choose to appreciate it even if you think it was only done out of politeness. It's the same way with women and a romantic man. You can appreciate being the object of his efforts even if you think he's doing it to impress himself, maybe, and even if he acted this way yesterday with another woman. You just have to take care not to make the mistake of thinking there's anything personal in it. You have to trust your common sense."

"Yes!" I pounced. "But that just seems like hypocrisy on his part and stupidity on hers, and I don't see how any self-

respecting woman would appreciate or even tolerate behavior
that makes her a dupe or a fool."

My wife laughed at me. Okay, I was unnecessarily worked
up. Was I jealous? Maybe seeing Barbara and Marcia get all
gooey about Antonio's smarmy blather made me feel unfairly
overlooked while trying to treat them as sensible human be-
ings. Here I'd spent many years earnestly toiling away at a brilliant symphony, so to speak, only to see my audience whoop
and holler and stamp their feet over some tv-ad ditty churned
out in an afternoon's conference by a gaggle of overpaid huck-
sters. The reward for my sincerity was to be ignored for it. We
men from the American West treat our women as equals; we
do not treat them as if they were swaddled in pink satin and
lace and as if they can't rise too quickly from the white wicker
chairs on their verandas without danger of swooning. We teach
them to shoot and to ride and to climb back up on that horse
when it throws them, goddangit. Our presumption of their
equality with us is the highest compliment we can bestow. We
do not like to see them horn-swoggled and love-swindled by
cheap and idle chatter. The whole idea is, well, foreign. I think
of Pepe LePew.

The next afternoon we went by Barbara's hostel to see if
she wanted to go with us to tour the old Moorish baths or the
Minaret of San Sebastian, but her evil old Señora told us she
hadn't seen her since the day before.

"Should we be alarmed?" I asked Marcia.

"I doubt it."

We left the next morning without seeing her again. We
went on to Granada, to Malaga, spent two weeks in Nerja, then

made a long rail haul to Barcelona. I thought of her off and on, a little worried about her welfare, but when we went to the American Express office in Barcelona for our mail, we found she'd left a note for us. I hadn't realized that this city was on her itinerary, but by now this kind of oddly miraculous intersecting had become something I almost expected.

We called the home of the friend she was staying with and met her that night at a cafe on the Ramblas down near the port.

We played Where You Been? for a few minutes and segued into Where You Going?, then I said, "Well, I was really glad to see you got out of Ronda unscathed."

She looked a little blank.

"Antonio."

"Uh, yeah," she laughed. "Antonio."

"We came by to see you, but we couldn't find you, and we started worrying that you'd been abducted," said Marcia.

She laughed. "Well, hardly."

She did spend that day with Antonio, she said. He borrowed a friend's mo-ped, and he took her riding out into the countryside. It was beautiful — the farms, the almond orchards in bloom — then he took her to the village where he lives. Lots of dogs in the street, you know, she remembered that. Some pigs, too. It had a little plaza in the center with a fountain where the women used to wash clothes before they all got running water. She made him take her to his house to meet his mother. His younger sister lives there, too, works in a *farmacia* on the plaza. His mother was one of those Spanish widow matrons who wore black shoes, black stockings, black skirt. She made a big lunch. What was it? Bean soup, pork chops and French fries. The sister had come home for siesta to eat. Did Barbara feel kind of like an exchange student? And was it interesting to be in somebody's house? Yes, she said. The mother made this incredible fuss over Antonio every minute while the younger sister sat and watched without smiling or saying very much.

"Maybe she resented having to work while he spent his time yakking in cafes all day long," I put in. "Maybe she thinks he ought to get a job."

Barbara shrugged. Anyway, she continued, after lunch the sister left and his mother took a nap. They went to Antonio's room. It was kind of like a monk's cell — a single bed, a small wooden desk, a throw rug, an old armoire. There was a plaster-of-Paris Virgin on the wall with a wire halo around her head. He had a little tape player. There was a poster over the desk for a suntan lotion, blonde in a maillot running out of the surf carrying a beach ball, she recalled. He was sweet, like a twelve-year-old boy with a weird crush on his teacher or something. He kissed her with his mouth closed.

"Have you written to him?" I asked.

"I lost his address."

"So was he a perfect gentleman after all?" asked Marcia.

"I don't know about that. He sure wanted not to have to be."

We all laughed.

"He said he wanted to marry me."

"Really? What'd you say?" I asked.

"I said I'd think about it."

"And have you?"

"Oh, he was harmless," she said with an air of utter dismissal. She might as well have added what woman wants a harmless man?

Poor Antonio, I thought with a laugh. Sitting alone in his room waiting and trusting that he'll get a letter that never comes, while the woman he adored goes on rambling and ambling from town to town, self contained, free as the wind. *La macha.* He sits alone as dusk fills up the room like a noxious gas. He'd made such effort trusting that she'd repay it with gratitude and allow him to be her foreign lover and maybe a husband. How could it mean so little to her? He stares at the plaster Mary, her glinting halo. He reaches to his jugular and unzips the yellow sweater to his wrist. It feels like his blood spills out.

Learning Inefficiency

Local customs provide needed therapy

Travel is an appropriately hellish torture for Type-A compulsives, but it's likewise good therapy. It's like that prescribed treatment said to cure you if it doesn't kill you first.

— In a supermarket in Florence, the line you're in stops creeping toward the checkout counter when the checker abandons her station to take her customer by the hand to search for an item at the back of the very large store. When you crane your head to estimate their progress down at the end of the long aisle, you see the customer is showing the checker some snapshots she's taken from her purse.

— You've set out to cash travelers' checks one morning in Granada. At the first bank, some people who might be tellers are drinking coffee and eating *churros* behind the counter, and after you've ahemed! them several times and made your request, one tells you that they don't do that here at this bank (sign on the door says otherwise). At the next bank, the sole visible occupant is wearing a cardigan sweater and blue jeans and sits smoking a Marlboro and staring meditatively off into space while steadfastly ignoring several customers who are lined at the counter just before him, and not a single waiting native admonishes him for skylarking. At the third bank, your teller cannot complete the transaction she's begun with you until after she takes care of the errand she is interrupted by her superior to run — to go buy a fistful of Once (lottery) tickets.

In Tavira, Portugal, I spent one entire day mailing a box back home. I offer following log as an exemplum:

8:30 — Arise in room of hostel *Residencial Lagoas Bica*, note breath condensing in the air, turn on toaster-sized electric heater, go back to bed.

9:00 — Get up again, put on shirt and pants and hover by your door waiting for the person presently using the communal shower to leave the bathroom down the hall, taking care not to blink because there's another person across the hall doing the same and you'll be beaten again to the buzzer, just like on "Jeopardy."

9:15 — Scurry into shower ahead of other person and pity him because, since you're third in line, you will use the remaining gallon of hot water. You were #4 yesterday. You live it up, gloat.

9:45 — Hair combed, shaved and shod, you climb to the rooftop terrace overlooking the Rio Gilao and the Mediterranean to see what kind of day it will be be: one or two layers? But since it has already turned out gloriously sunny and crisp, you sit for a while watching a flock of pigeons wheel and pirouette in the sky over red tile roofs below, the white undersides of their wings flickering like confetti in the sunlight. Far to the East over the ocean, a bank of cloud lies like the covers pushed to the foot of an unmade bed in the morning.

The pigeons come to roost in the belfry of the Church of the Misercordia on the hill above the town, and soon the bells ring for my gosh! is it —

10:00 — already? You go downstairs and finish dressing.

10:15 — Prepare and eat breakfast. This requires retrieving your skim milk from the refrigerator downstairs in the common room, hailing your cheerful Senhora with a hearty *"Bom Dia!"*, filling your coffee mug with Corn Flakes and milk, eating while idly perusing an old Herald Tribune spread on the bed for a tablecloth, then (this is like a camp breakfast — many steps even though the fare is simple), rinse your cup, fill it with water, put your immersion wand into it. As your water is heating, eat an orange and some Algarve figs bought yesterday at the market. When water in two cups is hot, prepare one cup of tea with milk and sugar for your mate and one cup of instant coffee with milk and sugar for yourself.

11:00 — Leave hostel to run errand of mailing a box of clothing back to the U.S. You peek into alleys looking for a cast-off box. If you were at home, you'd go to a liquor or drug store for it. You stroll across the Roman footbridge over the river Gilao and stop for a moment to admire the color scheme on Portugese fishing boats chugging downstream toward the estuary. You amble through the *Praca Da Republica* and its nearby *Jardim* on your way to the market, observing the duos and trios of old men strolling arm in arm along the *paseo*. Now and then the wing men hock a gleaming oyster onto the walk to mark their progress. You muse that they must have to shift positions now and then so that the middle fellow can safely hock left or right as they stroll. At the market you fail to find a box but you do see a black fish as long and as thick as your arm with a snout like a collie's and many rows of needle-sharp teeth, and another fish that looks like a basketball with an enormous, toothy Pac Man mouth, both just brought in from the nearby ocean. Shrimp, silvery sardines, fish as round and flat as the dinner plates they'll wind up on: born to be eaten! A smart three-legged dog looking both ways for mopeds before crossing the street. The images hang in your memory since your mind's not cluttered with plans to erect an empire.

11:45 — Boxless, you go to the official tourism office, where you wait your turn seated on an old couch and idly peruse a travel magazine in German, a language you don't know. (Second idle perusal of the day.) When you get the chance, you ask the helpful clerk in English where you might find a box. She says the post office sells them!

12:10 — A long line at the PO, but, heck, that can happen anywhere! A Portugese woman dressed in blindingly contrasting plaids appears to be trying to sell something to the only available clerk. When your turn eventually comes, you determine quickly that the clerk speaks no English, Spanish, or French, and has no apparent interest in learning any of these at this point in her life. Within seconds you have depleted your meager store of Portugese — Thank You! Excuse Me! Water! Please! Toilet! and, your personal favorite, Chicken! (*frango*) — so, using your arms, you convey your need for a box. You're shown various sizes. You select one — they come flattened — pay for it, and leave.

12:40 — You carry the box into a cafe and appreciate how its presence makes you look like a normal person having a normal life, and that means in these parts that you've got time to putz around on your way somewhere and that your empire won't miss you while you have a *bica* of coffee. So you order something normal — a *"bica"* of coffee, even if it does make you think of mud served in a thimble. Great taste, however. You have to down it in one gulp, like a shot of tequila. On a radio the Gipsy Kings are singing "Volare'" and high school girls at a nearby table chain smoke Marlboros while doing their homework. Funny that they're doing it In a cafe during what you think of as school hours. But then you're not in school or at work, either. The cafe is packed, and it's not lunch time by local measure.

12:55 — Return to room. Spend minutes marveling about the ingenuity of the design of this box: many slots and tabs, instructions in Portugese. You sit for a while and think of Christmas Eves spent assembling toys. Barbie Dream House, for example. When the box becomes a sturdy vessel, you fill it with a Portugese fisherman's sweater, some dead maps and guidebooks, a few souvenirs.

1:30 — Return to PO with box packed and addressed. You stand in line. The clerk inspects the box then keeps insisting upon something in Portugese, the thrust of which is that your box is being rejected, but you don't know why, and eventually the clerk, exasperated, looks over your shoulder to wait on the person behind you. A tall, elderly Englishwoman at the back of the line says, "You must tape it, too, I believe." That makes you feel at home.

1:45 — Take box to helpful clerk at the tourist office. She says that in Portugal one buys tape at a bookstore. Shows location of bookstores on map. Thank you, Turismo! *Muy obrigado!*

2:00 — Bookstore has just closed for a two and a half hour lunch. Sounds like a marvelous idea!

2:10 — Your own lunch at your favorite restaurant near your hostel follows: fresh bread and butter, a plate of olives, pate of salmon and spreadable cheese, vegetable soup, mixed salad, roasted *frango* and potatoes, a bottle of mineral water con gas, a carafe of wine, *puddim Molotov* (a custardy concoction, light and airy like a meringue), a *bica* of coffee. $10! There's a TV on the bar near your table that's playing an old episode of "The Rifleman," and in the interludes where normally commercials would be there are ancient film clips of The Sons of the Pioneers singing "Cool Water" and "Tumbling Tumbleweeds," songs you haven't heard since you were a kid way out West in the late 40s. You savor, savor these moments.

3:45 — Carrying box, you stagger to your room to nap. Used to be the Southern European habit of the mid-afternoon siesta was the world's most maddening interruption of consumer services to you, but now it seems like a solid chunk of ancient wisdom.

4:25 — Arrive at bookstore ten minutes early. Light a small cigar and sit in a nearby park with feet up on box watching English tourists with white hair, white hats, white shoes and pastel windbreakers stroll about. On your way back to the bookstore, you stop a minute to look through rusting iron gates into a monastery garden.

4:35 — Show the bookstore clerks your box, and they not only instantly understand what you need, they're quite willing to sell you only enough tape to do the job! Try that at Target! *Obrigado!*

4:40 — Back at the PO, the clerk accepts the box, weighs it, gives you a form to fill out. The form is in Portugese. Since noon the clerk still has not learned any language other than her native tongue, though lunch seems to have improved her disposition. Her expression conveys regret that between the two of you no further progress can be made.

4:55 — Arrive with box and form back at the tourist office, which, Thank God!, is close by. Your favorite clerk in all of Europe patiently translates directions on form and helps you fill it out. You make a mental note to write a "while I was traveling in your country" testimonial to the local newspaper, praising this young woman and asking that her salary be doubled.

5:10 — Back at the PO the clerk now gladly takes the box and the form, then she begins to leaf through several official-looking manuals apparently to learn what she is supposed to do at this point. A long line forms behind you, but no one mutters or appears to be fretting. That smart, three-legged dog trots by the door, stops, looks in, sniffs the air, goes on. The clerk disappears through a door for several minutes. When she returns, she writes down the cost (more than twice as much as lunch), you pay, she gives you a receipt, then says (big smile), *"Obrigado!"* to which you say, *"De Nada."*

5:30 — Rest in cafe near the riverside. Have a *copa* of *vino verde*, a Portugese specialty. Enjoy feeling of accomplishment, well-being. Have another *copa* to celebrate. Empires are built one stone at a time. Like the best art, they can't be hurried.

Views of the English at Oxford

Wondering if Mother knows best

Outside the library known as the Radcliffe Camera there's an odd bicycle rack — it's a little like an old concrete horse trough heaved up on its flank, and in what would normally be the bottom are deep grooves or slots in which a bike's front wheel will neatly chock.

According to a nearby sign, this rack is "Reserved for Readers Only." At the moment a dozen bikes are in their slips, their scholarly owners presumably huddled in the dim, piano-ivory light of the Camera at their seats, their eyes aching and their nostrils twitching from the mummy dust.

The nearest bicycle is a Raleigh with three speeds: 1) pretty easy, 2) a little harder, and 3) tough going if you're not whizzing along. It has old-fashioned handlebars shaped like gulls' wings, and its fenders have the patina of rust and paint, and the crinkled folds and dents, such as you see on old tobacco tins at flea markets. The frame and fenders were originally that deep burgundy of the Raleigh trademark, but now a grey scumble of time and English weather wash over the original color, and the wheel rims, spokes, and seat support, once glittering stainless chrome, now look like pewter. A wire basket hangs from the handlebars, fixed in place by twine; a plastic grocery sack is wrapped about the seat to keep it dry. The rubber on the tires shows open wounds. *Wash me*, this bicycle says. *Oil me. Paint me. Replace my arthritic hips and knees.*

This poor crippled thing is typical of the rest tilting wearily while forced to stand at parade rest in this rack; it's hardly distinguishable from its brethren. Though we see them being ridden all over Europe purely for transportation along the back roads of Portugal, Spain, and France, old bicycles seem to have their spiritual home in Oxford; I think it may be the Heaven where old bicycles go after they've been laid to rest.

Here they live a life of virtue among the virtuous. Even if there were no sign allowing the deduction that these are scholars' bicycles, it wouldn't take Inspector Morse to figure it out. A poor scholar would not have a new bicycle. Scholars at Oxford have a millennia-long reputation as threadbare bachelors living on bread and water — I'm thinking of Chaucer's clerk. For one thing, when you're studying, you're not devoting time to making a living or pursuing a vocation; for another, it costs to live while you're doing this.

Beside that old tradition of equating scholarship with poverty is another tradition of equating learning with deep preoccupation about matters of the mind and spirit, turning your back to the material world. All authorized scholars were, at one time, monks; Oxford was for century after century the place where aspirants to the clergy came to become. One thing they used to teach people who wanted to be Christians is that it's easier for a camel to pass through the eye of a needle than for a rich man to enter the Kingdom of Heaven. The reason is easy to see: for one thing, you have to rivet your mind to worldly things to become rich, and for another, you can only become rich by taking it from someone else, the amount of wealth on the planet being finite. The rich man thus commits two sins: he worries about only his own welfare, and he doesn't worry about the welfare of others — two sides to the same coin. The old Church Fathers always insisted that God didn't approve of such behavior.

We Americans have discovered an ingenious way of turning the doctrine inside out, so that now our televangelists constantly beseech us to see that wealth is how God shows his approval of our lives; therefore, the wealthy are the Chosen, their money's the very sign of it. Our bicycles, it follows, will always be state of the art, and we will not climb aboard them without first purchasing $300 worth of togs whipped up from space-age materials. Furthermore, we will be dedicated to only the most frivolous use of them — for cosmetically toning our muscles, for larking about on country roads in bands of a hundred or so — and this frivolous use is even further proof of our wealth.

In contrast, the Oxford scholar inside the Camera belongs to an ancient invisible fraternity of clerks and monks who, as I said, have been poor as a consequence of their choices or have taken a vow of poverty.

So to be an Oxford scholar is to wear the cloak and colors that identify members of the fraternity. Even if you could choose to tool about town on a $3000 kabillion-speed masterpiece of Japanese engineering rather than on this battered Raleigh, you wouldn't: displays of wealth are vulgar. They imply that you don't have your mind on proper things, that your values are shallow and materialistic.

Owning this Raleigh that is doubtless half a century old, you can abandon it at the doorway to wherever you're going without locking it up and without fear of its being stolen. It's amazing how the bikes of Oxford are like India's sacred cattle, protected from theft or molestation by a kind of religious force field. Not only are you protected by some would-be thief's lack of interest in the object, you're also insulated from theft by your own lack of worldly attachment to it — you're above caring if it's stolen. All is vanity, saith the Preacher.

This Raleigh's owner, bent over in seat 22 in the Camera, eyes watering, socks fallen down, collar askew and hair like Einstein's in that famous photo, is living out the legacy of Chaucer's clerk and countless ages of celibate and ascetic monks, even if she is reading Edmund Burke at the moment and not St. Augustine.

The ethos is clear: the more beat-up the bike, the better — the more it implies virtue in its owner.

Whoops! Seems I went the wrong way in the cheese line.

Here's what happened. I was on my best behavior otherwise with coat and tie because I'd been invited to have lunch at the Senior Common Room at St. Cross College by a nice bearded fellow from the Bodleian Library, and we'd been served a classic menu of roast beef, mashed potatoes, peas and Yorkshire pudding. Naturally, the peas were English. It was an English lunch. There was a good cabernet of which I had two (well, three) glasses, and I was feeling as if nobody was going to notice what an American clodhopper I was when I went and started down the wrong way in the cheese line.

It had been going pretty well. I insist on that I'd gotten all the way through lunch without belching or saying anything spectacularly stupid, and I was just about to congratulate myself for elevating myself in my host's eyes to the status of quasi-momentary-honorary Englishman. There were others of my American ilk there, too, and I could tell they were also a little uncertain whether they should eat their roast beef with their fork in their left hand or their right, too (or as the English say, "as well"), and so I know I'm not the only person in the world to have ever felt intimidated by being at table in the Mother country. After all, that's why it's called the Mother country, isn't it? The whole nation hovering over your shoulder watching your table manners and making your hair itch when you wear your gimme cap inside St. Paul's and giving you sort of shushing looks when you raise your voice to holler at your friend going down the street. The Mother country. It's got to be where Miss Manners takes her research leaves.

So I was just beginning to breathe a little easier about being human there in the Senior Common Room of St. Cross College amidst a herd of dons and two or three passels of scholars. I was beginning to feel more relaxed because I'd had that third glass of wine. This is one of those troublesome concepts. Feeling a need to feel at ease and afraid that you're going to do something terribly stupid and make a fool of yourself, you take that first glass of wine to relax, and then, relaxed, you take that second one because feeling relaxed feels pretty good and you might as well enjoy the feeling (especially since it's in such vivid contrast to what had been on your inner emotional pallet), and you relax enough to lose your fear of fumbling or stumbling or winding up like George Bush the Daddy puking into your Japanese host's lap.

I mean, drinking the second or even third glass of wine is sort of celebrating the fact that you've not made a fool of yourself yet by, say, going the wrong way in the cheese line. But then, sure enough, just when you're soused enough to let down your guard, well, whoops! there you go down the wrong-way street.

I plead ignorance. The cheese table was about the size of the stainless steel slabs they use in mortuaries for autopsies, and it stood about three feet from the wall. There was no sign saying This Way Only Through the Cheese Line. (Just like there's no sign at the High dinner table telling you that the port is to be passed only to your left. It has taken me years to understand that the English have three billion rules for being English and they're not published anywhere, because, I suspect, the English don't really want just anybody to learn how to be English.)

Anyway, I picked up a plate from the cheese table then mosied along inspecting the laid-out goods, circled around the far end — this would be turns #1 and #2 in the Indianapolis 500 — then I came poking along the backstretch and got interested in stopping off at the Brie and the Stilton, which, as everyone knows, is a famous English cheese. It seemed a good way to top off a meal of English peas and Yorkshire pudding.

The method for getting cheese and crackers on your plate seemed cumbersome. While holding a plate in one hand, you have to take a dull knife in your other and attempt to hack slivers or chunks from a wheel that's loose on a plate and tends to skid about when you apply any pressure to it, and you're not supposed to make a mess or leave the cheese looking like five-year olds had used it for an art project. You can get a master's degree in the proper way to carve cheese at the Sorbonne, and believe me, I can testify firsthand that if you do it wrong, a French person will let you know. Being American, I opted merely for efficiency and thereby made a crumbly mess. I missed America all of a sudden, where the hostess serves cheese diced and stacked in cubes like Lego cities, and you can spear it with toothpicks and the like.

Well, I finally got some, less than I would've gotten if I could've dug or cut it out with ease and dispatch, and was sauntering toward the Finish line when I almost ran head-on into some English people waiting for me to cross the ribbon.

It was a man and a woman slightly behind him. They were dressed after the fashion of homeless people, only in tweeds, and so I knew immediately that they were doubtless renowned scholars of something, with international reputations to boot. They stood with bemused smiles, plates pressed to their bosoms as if to deflect spears and arrows.

"Oh, my God!" I'm afraid I gushed. "I'm going the wrong way."

The fellow — he was taller than I and his glasses were considerably older — wrinkled his scholarly brow as if musing or meditating, and finally said, "Well, it's not the wrong way, you know. It's only that we're rather in the custom of going the other way."

"Yes, truly," piped up the woman at his elbow. "It really doesn't matter so long as we don't all bump noggins now, does it?"

The fellow turned to her. "Certainly not. It's habit, that's all."

He seemed to have stopped addressing me and was sort of taking up the subject as an object of contemplation between them. It was a little as if they'd been arguing about it all morning, and he wanted to get in the last word here.

In any case, they both smiled pleasantly at me, and stepped aside to let me pass.

Now that I look back upon it, how they coped with the alarming spectacle of someone going the wrong way in their cheese line pleased me, gave me a warm feeling about these English. They wanted me to feel OK. They're ok, I'm ok. They didn't try to tell me I'd done something wrong, and they didn't try to favor their favorite direction by arguing that it was somehow intrinsically more sensible. They let me off the hook by making themselves look capricious and arbitrary. They didn't try to excuse me on the grounds of ignorance, or "forgive" me and indulge me this once. What they said was that one way to go is just as good as another.

The English have a well-deserved reputation for politeness all over the planet Earth. But politeness doesn't mean friendliness — I've seen several snickering references in English newspapers to the American habit of commanding customers to have a nice day — and it doesn't mean that they necessarily care about you or want you to engage in conversation with them. This is the way they treat one another — respectfully, with a little distance. You know the old sociological saw about how different cultures put a differing measure of literal space between faces when talking to one another? The Italians and Spanish about fifteen centimeters, the French a few more, and so forth? The English like to keep a good two feet between themselves and the next face, and that's an ancient English way of measuring, anyway. I've always wondered if that's not why they're so famous for respecting places in a line: to cut into a line, you have to half that gap of comfort between yourself and the next fellow.

We, on the other hand, believe that we have to smile and engage strangers in conversation to qualify as "nice" people. But to the English, forcing someone else into unnecessary or excessive intercourse is in itself a species of rudeness. And here I've got in mind those poor, caught-in-the-middle waitpersons in the U.S. whose managers have told them they must insist on being called by their first names by diners. To the rest of the world, knowing one's waiter by any name would be an absurd presumption, and having to be introduced to him or her as a condition of placing a meal order would be a preposterous imposition upon the diner's and the waiter's privacy.

When we got on the London tube late one night, the train lurched a moment, then stopped, and the voice of the motorman came over the intercom. "Ladies and gentlemen," he said. "It seems I have a red light at the moment. That must mean another train ahead is still on the track. I'm terribly sorry for the inconvenience. If we don't get a green light within a few short moments, I'll try to check on what might be the difficulty. Again, I'm terribly sorry for the delay." A beat, then — "Oh! Well! I see it's green again! We'll be off now. Cheers!"

One night we're invited to an occasion where the guest of honor gives a talk and tells us all he's "the four hundred and thirty-seventh mayor of Abingdon," as well as being a former president of the local Rotary. He's got something draped around his neck that looks to me like — given my poor eyesight and the post-sherry haze in the room — either a throttled peacock or a garland made of mice wearing sunglasses. But when he rattles it, I see it's actually a ceremonial necklace that symbolizes like a monarch's scepter one of those two aforementioned offices, though I never understand which.

What really strikes my ear is this "four hundred and thirty-seventh" business. This seems to be our week for this sort of thing. Only a few days before, I heard another fellow who heads up Oxford University's Bodleian Library describe himself as "Thomas Bodley's twenty-second librarian," and then he went on and zipped back to 1620 or so to tell us about the very first one. I had a feeling that he could've named the other twenty-one in their proper order.

I'm astonished that these fellows see themselves as standing at the head — or would that be the foot? — of a very long queue, as it were. Would you say that they're at the bottom or top of it, at the beginning or the end? That's really the question, isn't it — whether thinking of yourself that way would be a help or a hindrance as you poked along in your doggy little life perpetuating the multiplicity of quaint traditions and obligations, customs and rituals involving sacred objects such as the peacock festooning this Abingdon fellow's neck. Such a burden of history to keep up!

Experimenting with the idea, I try to think of myself as my university's fourth Professor of Creative Writing, but since two of the other three are still living as colleagues on the spot, somehow the sense of the baton passing to me just isn't there. Once I was President of a fifty-year-old club of writers, and, taking the gavel, I was informed that it was always a tradition (how could it have been "always" a tradition?) that the President bring to each meeting a quart of Jack Daniels black to set on the conference table. I dutifully did this only to discover that no one drank any, so I brought it one more time, then henceforth conveniently "forgot" to bring it, since it was a nuisance to drag it out and dust off the shoulders of the bottle, carry it to the car, etc. That's about the closest I can come to in finding a comparison in my own life with being Bodley's twenty-second or Abingdon's four-hundred and thirty-seventh, and I obviously was careless in duties, few as they were.

"And each year hence..." X or Y has happened. Traveling in England you can hear this semantical structure uttered by docent after docent. The mayor of Oxford has to prostrate himself upon the steps of some building annually as penance for a peasant uprising against the university's scholars way back when; the English monarch has to ask formal permission from the Lord Mayor to enter the City of London; each year on a particular May at 6 a.m., a choir climbs to the top of Oxford's Magdalen College Tower to sing, and so forth.

Docents and guides stress the idea of repetitive commem-
orative acts in briefing tourists on English history, giving you
the idea that this is what it means to the English to be English
— "tradition." You get the idea that English life consists of acts
that must be repeated annually or biannually or every hour
on the half hour. This would seem to make English life rather
thick with acts that do not step forward, so to speak (you could
say the minute hand moves but the hour hand does not), and
it makes a place like Oxford seem to hang forever in a haze of
the past. New buildings (such as the "New" library) are uni-
versally abhorred unless they look like the old ones, in which
case they are only objects of mild contempt for being mere rep-
licas or counterfeits, like parvenus trying to buy their titles.
The proliferation of dramas by Shakespeare in college quads
takes on the character of ancestor worship, to say nothing of
the busy chamber groups airing out the music of respectably
dead composers. A trip through Westminster Abbey is a stroll
through a mausoleum where stone coffins stacked atop each
other bear the bones of English kings and queens, many of
whom, it seems, strangled, quartered, hanged or stabbed one
another with distressing regularity, and the weight of all that
stone, all that sorrow, all that melancholy plainsong passing
in the mind's ear like a chilly wind...well, that is a burden, is it
not? It's not too far removed from learning that there's been a
long string of suicides in your family history: how's that going
to make you greet the day?

The veneration of history, of tradition, gives people a sense
of identity, but it likewise fixes their feet in concrete. If everything must be justified by precedent, how does something new
come into being? Sue Bridehead in Thomas Hardy's *Jude the*

Obscure calls Oxford "a nest of commonplace schoolmasters whose characteristic is timid obsequiousness to tradition." Preserving the past means also preserving the mistaken presumptions, the folly-making notions and utterly preposterous convictions of your forebears, such as those poor Jude faces when he finally, after working for many years preparing himself for life as a scholar, reaches the city of Oxford. Finding a job as a stone mason, he continues to study on his own and applies for entry to one of the colleges only to be informed by its master that he would be better off staying in his own class, among his own kind. In a bitter fury of depression, he drowns his sorrows in umpteen pints of bitter, scrawls "I have understanding as well as you!" on a college wall, rails against the dons of "Sarcophagus College" and the like, then he slinks back to his native village in defeat and humiliation.

This makes me think of the fellow in my clan who first came to America from England. Significantly, I don't know who he was, because neither he nor his immediate progeny were remotely interested in keeping track of this sort of thing. It might be he couldn't read or write. But he also might have been a Jude who, in a fit of pique and wounded pride, crawled off to the hold of a leaky privateer bound for the New World rather than back to his luckless barren history in the old one.

So the idea of America begins for me in how you flee from history, not embrace it. For me, American to the core, being Bodley's twenty-second would only mean having to do what Bodley's other twenty-one did (well, you could do it better, of course), and the small slot reserved for you in the bicycle rack of history would guarantee you a place, of course, but you'd always be the same distance from the door, for better or worse.

That garland, that necklace on the bosom of Abingdon's Four Hundred and Thirty-seven Mayor, conjures many other images; I think of the Ancient Mariner and his albatross, that burden of past transgressions. I think of neckties and the formality and distinctions of class they represent, how they constrict and choke. Last but not least, there's the noose and the gallows from which it hangs.

Home on the Range

Encountering a specter of homelessness

Thanks and No Thanks to Paulette Torassa, that nice French girl who showed up in our high school as an exchange student, I started seeing life in my small New Mexico town through her eyes, and I knew I wanted to stay in a foreign person's home someday. Get to see the way those people really live, you know.

Paulette also taught me the word *pension*, and I was swept up by the romantic idea of it, how some day when I traveled overseas I could stay in a charming hotelette owned and run by down-at-heels aristocrats who'd been forced by bad luck or a revolution to turn their ancestral home into rooms rented to eccentric exiled princes, starving students in berets, and irascible spinster-novelists or aging bachelors, all of whom would form an agreeable but intriguing melange during dinners presided over by an elderly host clad in a mothy tuxedo that reeked of Old World decay. There'd be tarnished silver and heirloom china showing chips and hairline cracks, cigars and espresso.

I'd grown up with "Leave It To Beaver" dinners served at 5:30 when my Dad came home from work, dinners featuring such staples as pot roast accessorized by Wonder Bread and Parkay margarine and Jell-O salads, so to say the word "pahn-see-own" softly to myself was to conjure up other words I'd read but never had the opportunity to use — "con-see-erjuh" and "demi-tasse," or "cap-oo-cheeno," or "AHN-tray." I'd heard of something called "crepes Suzette" and didn't know what they were, but to my American boy's mind, it seemed fitting that a French dish should have such an oo-la-la name.

I had a lot to unlearn. For one thing, I'd presumed that these hapless proprietors would be happy to have us around; for another, I'd imagined that their quirks would be amusing entertainment purchased at no expense to my comfort or happiness. I also had no idea just how important it would be in traipsing from one European town to another for six months and living out of a single suitcase that the room where you're staying should offer a comfortable, pleasant, and safe refuge from the wolfish world beyond the door.

In Madrid, our first stop, we'd been fairly lucky. "Mr and Mrs. Pedro" — or so we called them — were short and stocky workhorses with a fetish for cleanliness that led them to dash into the bathroom after anyone had used it for any reason and give all the porcelain fixtures a hearty hosing like the firefighters in asbestos outfits do at Cape Canaveral. They'd swab down the tile floors, then they'd fling open the windows that you'd closed so that the icy January gale wouldn't chill your shower water, which was, anyway, only a tepid trickle to begin with. For twenty bucks a night you didn't get heat but for a couple hours in the evening, when it eked weepingly from a radiator whose valves had been painted over many times. Mr. and Mrs.

Pedro's mania for cold and cleanliness made us suspect that they suspected us of harboring unspeakably vile diseases.

But shivering in an antiseptic environment was preferable to what we encountered in Seville. The *Hostal-Residencia de los Reyes* (the only place of the affordable six called from the *turismo* office with a vacancy) was down a dark cobblestone alley so narrow you could touch the buildings on both sides at once. A dark foyer off the alley had a wrought-iron gate that let onto a patio dim as someplace in Atlantis, an effect resulting from how the atrium over it rose three stories to an opening that had been covered by plastic roofing, and that, in turn, was blanketed by leaves. Looking up into it, you thought of a light fixture with a layer of dead bugs in it, only the size of a circus tent.

A woman who might have been a Polish farmer's wife answered our ring wearing an apron, stockings rolled to her ankles, and an expression that said we represented more floors to mop and beds to make.

She was holding a bucket. We presumed that she used it to clean the bathrooms. We were wrong. In our stay neither the bathroom floors nor the commodes, bidets, sinks, tub or shower would get her attention. That bucket was for her to use in endlessly scrubbing three narrow flights of marble stairs that were the last extant sign of the nobility claimed in our guidebook entry describing this pahn-see-own as "housed in a former ducal residence." No matter what time of night or day we needed to go up or down those stairs, there she'd be like a character from a fairy tale, on her hands and knees, kneading her rags, scrubbing, scrubbing as if a terrible hellish spell had been cast upon her. She wouldn't acknowledge our waiting presence above or below her until we murmured, *"Perdon, Señora, por favor,"* and then she'd grunt and groan to her feet and stand aside not speaking or looking at us as we passed.

A younger woman who seemed equally unhappy with her lot in life negotiated with us for rooms. For a night, fifteen bucks, without bath, two dollars extra for a little electric heater (gladly!). Towels and sheets changed once a week. You may not call out on the telephone. If you have further questions, don't ask them.

In the communal kitchen upstairs, two American students were cooking their nightly portions of pasta and vegetables using unmatched cookware that reminded us of college days. One was washing dishes in a very greasy sink using a whiskey-colored sponge that was shredding off into the dishwater. A window near the girl's head looked out onto an airshaft where sewer pipes grumbled and leaked from an upstairs flushing.

While they worked the girls were receiving the attention of a man we presumed to be a homeless wino whom the girls had once, regrettably and foolishly, lavished their compassion upon. He was a monkey of a man, face rutted like a raisin, and he had bald patches in his scalp that hinted of whole dead zones in his skull. His eyeglasses were so smudged with fingerprints that I wondered if he weren't blind. He was wearing a stained suit coat over a filthy cardigan; he was smoking a dark Ducado, a cheap Spanish cigarette with a particularly weedy stench. He dropped ashes all over his sleeves and onto the table where we were spreading our ham and cheese to fix sandwiches. He hovered behind and beside the girls as they worked, cackling, cooing, drooling, leering. The girls smiled over their shoulders like nervous flight attendants.

Soon another fellow popped in, a slight fellow in tight pants and a rose-colored shirt worn over a white turtleneck. He announced that he'd just cut his hair. He pirouetted to show off his do, a winged creation faintly reminiscent of the one Farrah Fawcett made popular years ago on "Charlie's Angels."

The old man left to go to the bathroom, and the fellow with the new hairdo likewise drifted away. The girls told us that the latter was a permanent resident of the hostel. The old "wino" was, they said, the husband to the *duenna*, the landlady, the stair-scrubber herself. Rather than fix the dozens of broken locks, windows, doors, and rather than putty, scrape, or paint, or remount the dangling light fixtures or sweep the leaves off the atrium dome, the lord and master of this domain lurked all day below waiting for the kitchen light to go on up here so he could come hobbling in like Quasimodo to sniff the air around where the girls were standing.

When we left the kitchen we went down the hall to the bathroom we shared with other upstairs rooms, and we discovered where the other fellow had practiced his beautician's craft: the sink was full of wet black clippings, hunks and hanks of hair. His *amigo*, the old man, had apparently taken a piss in the commode without raising the lid, and you'd have to wipe his yellow splatter off the seat before you could sit down. He didn't bother to flush, either. His last act before leaving the bathroom had been to hawk up a gleaming oyster into the bottom of the bidet. (The penchant of Iberian men for hawking and spitting had already given us one running gag: that the Spanish translation of Dickens' famous novel was entitled, "Great Expectorations.")

Few hostels were that bad. Almost all were bitter cold, but

most were clean, and many were pleasant. Between Madrid and Sevilla there'd been a week in Lisbon at the amply heated *Residencial Aleluia* run by an amiable Senhora who gave us this mild warning against youthful pickpockets at the flea market: "Small boys take! No kill, only take!" In Evora, Portugal, we found, cheap, a beautifully appointed room with a bathtub seven feet long, and though the room had no heat, there was unlimited hot water, and we'd fill the tub, climb in with our peanut butter sandwiches, and soak until we were warm. In Tavira, Portugal, our cheerful and energetic Senhora at the *Residencial Lagos Bica* gave us an electric heater for a tile-floored room that let out onto a terrace overlooking the town and the port, and she unfailingly offered up a happy *"Bom Dia!"* each time we'd see her.

In Cordoba we were among the first guests at the *Hostal Alcazar*, run by Sr. and Sra. Roberto Muñoz, a young couple who'd just started up their business after Sr. Muñoz had left a job as a publicist for a match manufacturer. Anxious to please, Sr. Muñoz served us breakfast in a coat and tie, fired up the electric brazier under the breakfast table, and we'd drape the tablecloth over our laps and toast our legs and feet while he tried jokingly and without success to get their Pekingese "Sophia Loren" (because she'd been bred to a dog named "Carlo Ponti") to do tricks. He introduced us to his two grammar-school kids, and, after he and his wife had seen the son and daughter off to school at the front gate (this was always oddly comforting to witness, as he shook their hands with a mock formality and she kissed them), the Señora would settle down to a morning of cleaning the rooms and singing contentedly and unselfconsciously the Moorish airs she'd learned as a girl growing up in a nearby village.

You pay for your enjoyment of one place by your treatment at the next. It was a kind of tax. Our last stop before pushing on to Italy was Nice, where we had quite a grand old time, and that meant — we knew this even as we were taking enormous pleasure in our stay in Nice — that the dues ahead would be heavy.

We hit a string of bad luck. In Pisa, Marcia invented another rule: if your guidebook says the rooms in the hostel feature ancient frescoes, avoid it at all costs. That really means high ceilings in an old stone building where there has been no heat since some Duke torched his wife or his enemies in the fireplace centuries ago.

We arrived during a cold rain that made Florence seem brutal and somber and trudged with our bags for two hours from one too-expensive hostel to another (including the one overlooking the Arno used for some filming of "A Room With a View"), until at last, with both of us on the verge of sobbing from the cold, from weariness, from hunger, we settled on a place five minutes' walk from the *Piazza della Repubblica* and the major museums. It was also near the *Palazzo Vecchio*, before which Savanarola and his followers had lighted their famous bonfire in 1497 to destroy "vanities" that symbolized the corruption of the times (jewelry, playing cards, bawdy pictures, gaming tables), a fabled act I got a new slant on when I realized that the freezing citizenry could at least warm their hands and feet during the delightful duration of it.

We had a clean and large but unheated room in a hostel run
by a gay couple, the less taciturn of whom we called Leonardo
di Baldy. Leonardo apologetically explained that we couldn't
use the shower down the hall near our room because the hot
water took too long to reach it (in other words, we couldn't use
it because it worked), and he was very upset when we tripped
a breaker to the entire building by merely plugging in an immersion wand to heat a cup of water for tea. Two midnights
running some fellow just across the courtyard kept us awake
while he screeched for an hour at someone who never talked
back. When we complained, Leonardo tsk-tsked in sympathy
for the poor fellow: he was screaming over the phone at his
estranged wife's lawyer.

Trying to escape the cold, we went out into the drizzle
(that's backwards, no?) and set about dutifully to be tourists
hoping at least that walking and thinking and looking at
cathedrals and paintings might take our minds off being
cold. (Besides, wasn't site and art-seeing our job, as tourists?)
We hadn't frozen, of course, and we hadn't suffered frost-
bite. These were voluntary privations, too. But it seemed that
for weeks we'd not been anywhere inside or out where the
temperature was over 58 degrees or so, and that chill had
seeped far down into our souls.

Outside our uninviting hostel, Florence was curiously
uninviting, the streets narrow and grey and dirty and dark,
with high walls of damp grey stone and noisy traffic, and the
cold bare piazzas had absolutely no greenery or benches. What
seemed particularly heartless was that the city offered no chair
to ease weary feet that didn't have to be rented by a ticket
to a museum or an order placed in a restaurant. Florentines

seemed aware that their distant ancestors once had produced some definitive signs of a truly graceful civilization, but they themselves had long since lost the knack of how it's done, and all they could do now was to exploit it. They turned their most central piazza — the *Piazza della Repubblica* — into a parking lot and four-way thoroughfare.

Our spirits sank lower and lower. Seething, I did a mental remake of "A Room With a View," which, in some vague way, I blamed for my disappointment and discomfort:

1. A Room With A View Of A Dark And Dingy Courtyard.

2. A Room With A View Of A Dark Courtyard Where Every Night Between Midnight And One A.M. You Can Hear A Guy Screaming Insanely At His Ex-wife's Lawyer On The Phone.

3. A Room With A View Of A Piazza That's Been Turned Into A Parking Lot And A Thoroughfare For One Million Mufferless Mopeds.

4. A Room With A View Of A Large And Paved Piazza Without A Single Park Bench Or Scrap Of Green In The Form Of Tree Bush Or Potted Plant.

5. A Room With A View Of A Piazza Where A Cafe Has Outdoor Seating If You Don't Mind Paying Five Dollars For A Cup Of Coffee Or A Glass Or Water.

6. A Room With A View Of A Shower Down The Hall You Are Instructed Not To Turn On Because It Uses Hot Water.

7. A Room With A View And A Sink That Has Warm Water In It Only After It Has Been Running For Half An Hour.

8. A Room With A View And A Very Strictly Enforced Policy Of No Laundering And The Laundromats Charge Fifteen Dollars A Load.

9. A Room With A View And An Electrical Outlet You Thought You Could Use To Plug In Your Immersion Wand To Make A Cup Of Tea Until Doing So Made All The Lights In The Hostel Go Out And The Owner Told You To Never Never Do That Again In This Hotel.

But (wouldn't you know), on Saturday the sun heaved itself out of hibernation and we ambled across the Arno on the *Ponte Vecchio* and found the Boboli Gardens above the *Palazzo Pitti* and the grassy slope just under the *Citadel Belvedere*, where we lay in the sun drinking wine for the afternoon with a great view of the Campanile and the Duomo across the Arno, then we found a cheerful, solidly proletarian restaurant on the *Via Della Spada* where we gorged family-style on fettucini with red sauce, pork ribs, salad, bread and much more wine in big jugs at a table we shared with a workingman in those ubiquitous royal-blue coveralls and his toddling son, who, as children always do, unwittingly played ambassador and go-between for all of us. We liberally applied all our available Italian — *scuze, prego, bella bella bella, bene, bono, molto bene, per favore, tutti, buona sera, bambino* — and learned not surprisingly that our companion had a relative in New York.

Suddenly the Florentines were hospitable and charming and their city glowed yellow in the sun. When events such as those would lift my spirits, it would make my earlier black mood seem oddly mythic or tinted with the romance of the literary, and I'd equate my tourist's discomforts with those fabled privations artists endured during the 20s and 30s in Paris. When the rain stopped and the front had passed, the sun shone fitfully for a couple of days, and Leonardo di Baldy's carping about washing our socks in the sink didn't irritate me because I could walk out of the gloomy room and stroll about the city with pleasure.

"Where should we stay in Roma?" we'd asked travelers we'd met in Barcelona who'd just come from there. Would they recommend their hostel? She said, "Ummm," and he said, "Well, uh, yeah, I guess."

"What's wrong with it?"

"Well, nothing, really," he said. "It's clean and cheap."

"Cold," said the wife.

"Sure," her spouse said — what else was new?

"Tell them about Franco," she said.

"Who's Franco?" asked Marcia.

"He's the guy who runs the place. He likes to tease people."

"Curse at them is more like it."

"Well, yeah, he kind of cusses you out, you know? But he doesn't mean anything by it."

"What do you mean?"

"Well, like John Cleese on 'Fawlty Towers.'"

"Only not funny," snorted his wife.

"How'd you find out about it?"

The place wasn't in *Let's Go* — he found it in Becker's, he said. He could show me the listing. According to the Johnathan Becker guidebook, the loquacious Franco and his lovely Rhodesian wife Augusta were the extraordinarily helpful hosts at their exceedingly tidy hostel. Becker's way of handling the issue of the landlord's persona was an additional note that said Franco "is as full of information as he is personality gained from his former acting career."

I should have heard alarm bells from the tepid advisory alone or when my recommender said Franco's place was listed only in Becker's. My experience with guide books thus far had led me to doubt if "Johnathan Becker" existed, or, if he did, he probably hadn't made a personal visit to any listing in twenty years, and, if he had, they knew he was coming: *Whoa, here comes Johnathan Becker — turn on the water heater and the radiators, change out those 15-watt bulbs!*

Ignoring all warnings, I made a reservation that night in Barcelona for Franco's Roman *pensione*. I must have talked to the lovely Rhodesian wife, Augusta.

What're my excuses? This came before our string of bad luck in Italy and before the cold had ground us down, and I'd been intrigued by the description of Franco — I thought maybe at last I'd found a "real" hostel, one with a pervasive air of attractive eccentricity, the true value of which my advisors had failed to appreciate.

Franco had the faintly simian look of a clean-shaven gorilla, and said, when we showed up to sign in after schlepping our bags seven blocks from the *Stazione Termini*, "Nice to have you. Now get out of my fucking way. I love you. Go stand over there."

He made us wait at parade rest while he whisked away the stack of folded towels from the desk and lumbered out of sight down a hallway with them. The building was in a decidedly dubious neighborhood, and we'd had to enter by buzzing up. You stepped off the elevator at the fourth floor into this entry, which, like many such "lobbies," was only a chock of hallway furnished by a desk and a couch that, for lack of knee-room, couldn't be set against the wall directly in front of it.

A bulletin board behind the desk honored Franco's "career" in show biz — there was an 8 X 10 glossy of him in a loin cloth and headdress and war paint but showing his huge barrel chest (apparently a still from a spaghetti western), another series with him among other players clad in wigs and knee-breeches. The centerpiece of the display was a full-page ad for Ietley's tea clipped from a magazine, showing a restaurant scene, Franco in a red waiter's jacket bending over a table, teapot in hand, smiling into the camera, and the copy, in English, said, "Giancarlo knows how to make the best tea in Italy."

When he came back and flung himself down behind the desk to take our passports and sign us in, I said, just to suck up, "So you're also an actor?"

"Who knows? Who cares? I'm too busy to talk. Here." He gave us keys he identified as fitting the downstairs door, the elevator, the *pensione's* front door, our own door. I must have looked puzzled. Exasperated, he said, "I lock up from midnight to seven-thirty. I can't come running all the time for you fucking people. Let yourself in and out. I trust you. I love you. I like Japanese, Americans, Germans, English, Australians. I don't take backpackers or Arabs or Africans. Nobody from the Third World and never Italians. I hate fucking Italians. I can't be worrying all the time about somebody knocking me in the head at night." He bolted out of the chair. "Now get out of my fucking way, I'm busy." When he breezed by Marcia, he suddenly flung his arms about her and gave her a rib-cracking hug. "I love you, bella!" He kissed her several times on the cheek, and I thought of the "Saturday Night Live" routine involving Kirstie Alley and a crew of waiters in an Italian restaurant. "And you," he turned to me. "I love you too."

"Thank you," I said. "Would you happen to have a map of Rome handy?"

"Map? Do I look like the tourist bureau? No, I don't have maps. Now leave me alone. I love you."

He cocked his head the way a dog or cat will when suddenly hearing something vitally important you or I cannot, then unexpectedly dashed off. I presumed he'd return shortly to show us our room. I looked at Marcia, and we grinned. He was on, and talking to him gave me that same nervous but stimulating sensation you have when you sit first row at a play known to involve audience participation. Likewise, his kidding banter, his bluster, seemed safely theatrical, a mask he would (surely) drop if you needed however momentarily to be someone other than a passive and supposedly appreciative audience.

We waited five, ten minutes. I searched among the fistful of keys for one with a room number, thinking that maybe he'd expect us to find it ourselves. The charm of being treated with the same jocular contempt with which we were spoken to quickly wore thin, though, and I was about to lead us off into a maze of hallways when a tall, big-boned woman with a very sober expression stepped off the elevator behind us. Her way of acknowledging that we were perhaps guests of the *pensione* was to seat herself behind the desk then merely favor us with her gaze, as if to observe idly from an al fresco cafe while we did something mildly engaging at the curb. She was Yin to Franco's Yang. This turned out to be Augusta, the lovely Rhodesian wife.

I explained that we'd checked in — here I rattled the keys above my head as if showing off a pelt — but hadn't yet been shown, well seen, our room. She glanced at the book, uttered a number, then pointed down the hall and said, "Only lefts."

The first left took us past a large dining room with windows overlooking the street, the second past what appeared to be a laundry room through whose door we spied Franco with a portion of white sheet tucked between his chin and chest while he struggled to fold the rest of it like a sailor bringing in a spinnaker. We waved as we went by, and he yelled, "Hello. Welcome. Don't come in here and don't ask me nothing. I don't have time to talk to you. Go away."

The final left took us past a partially opened door that revealed the skinny shanks and knobby knees of some person seated on a commode. Thinking we'd somehow caught someone by surprise, we gave each other a ???!!! look and tried to tiptoe past the door to spare the poor soul embarrassment, but a gaseous howl from the porcelain hollow made us titter aloud.

Our room was large and clean but dark and chilly. Above the sink was the room's sole light fixture with a 25-watt bulb mounted over the mirror and sink like a single horn. Behind old Venetian blinds were two milky windows facing the inner courtyard; they were covered with a lattice of diagonal burglar bars, and beyond that scaffolding hooded them. The courtyard was a vast jumble of brick and board, piles of sand, construction debris.

The workers arrived at 6:30 the next morning and the first tool they reached for was, naturally, a jackhammer. Now and then the operator was forced to stop, but only because hammering interfered with his bellowing at someone two dozen yards away who stood atop the scaffold just outside our window.

Franco served breakfast from 8 to 9. At 7:50 several

Germans, English, and Americans who had restrained themselves from knocking Franco in the head during the night were standing in the hall outside the closed door of the dining room checking and rechecking our watches while we listened to Montovani-styled violins swelling from a radio inside and to the bumping screech of chair legs on a linoleum floor.

Franco came rushing along, shouting, "Out of my fucking way, goddamnit!" to us. He was carrying a tray of white crockery. "What are you all standing out here for?" For an instant, I thought this was his way of inviting us to open the door and go inside, but, no, he then said, "I serve from eight to nine, eight to nine! Look at your watches!" meaning that it wasn't his fault we had to wait in the hallway.

When he reached the door, he hollered, "Goddamnit, don't be stupid! Somebody open the fucking door!" When someone did, he said, "That's it. Thank you, moron! I love you!"

He kicked the door shut behind him in our faces. We all laughed, a little uneasily. Yesterday I'd thought all this was kidding, but this would-be parody of a gruff innkeeper seemed this morning like a handy way to disguise real hostility. Acting the role of the irascible innkeeper of Fawlty Towers then pretending it was only a role — letting the seams show, as it were — allowed him to vent his unhappiness of being one? And "I love you" was just to disarm you?

"I wonder what's for breakfast?" someone asked, laughing.

"Turd fritters," I said.

"And you'll like them, too," added Marcia.

"Turd fritters" was our running joke about hostel-proprietor hospitality, but Franco's breakfast turned out to be tasty and substantial, and, unlike other innkeepers of Southern

Europe, he understood, just as the ad said, that "tea" in English was not a glass of hot milk with cinnamon and a splash of liqueur made from, say, artichokes.

He personally served several tables of us ("You want chocolate, coffee, or tea? Make up your fucking mind!") — soft-boiled egg, fresh crusty rolls, butter and lockets of cheese and jam to which we added an orange we'd bought at the market. ("How come you bring that? You think I don't feed you enough? Go eat somewhere else!")

Mid-meal I looked up to see a person clinging to the wall near the door like a chameleon. A tall, very thin woman of indeterminate age clad in a wool knit skirt and sweater and beret all of the same jolly-green hue was shuffling along the baseboard toward the nearest table, ours. Stroke victim, I thought. Her skin said she was over 70, but her hair was still red and worn in a 60s "flip" with bangs streaked with grey that set aside suspicions of a wig.

I rose and pulled out the chair at our table nearest her, and she took it slowly and calmly as if we'd planned this.

She told us her name, but we eventually took to calling her "Blanche" behind her back. Only one side of her mouth worked fully, but she didn't slur. She had clear green eyes and high cheekbones and must have been beautiful in her youth, a supposition we drew also from her vanity: she wore false eyelashes and mascara and a brilliant red lipstick too large for her mouth — now and then her drawing hand had obviously taken a loopy detour.

As we anted up our first names, Franco brought her a pot of coffee.

"No more tea," he said as he set it down and stepped away.

"I don't drink coffee!" she hurled at his back.

"Learn," he said.

She turned to us. "Rudest goddamn man I ever met."

"He's certainly volatile," I said.

She snorted. "Typical Southern Italian. I'd bet his family was Gypsy. He told me his mother 'marked' him —" here she gestured to her ribcage — "before they were separated in a refugee camp during the war, so she could always recognize him. He said she never did find him later. I doubt that she tried. I think she'd probably sold him."

She'd been enduring his insults for six weeks, she said. I wondered why but didn't ask. She said she'd been in Rome two years. When she lifted her cup and slurped at the coffee without apparently noticing or caring that it wasn't tea, you could see that her knuckles were knobbed from arthritis.

Without our prompting, she offered a cameo biography while painstakingly tearing a roll into bits such as you might use to feed pigeons and attempting to butter them. She said she'd come to Italy to be a writer. "It was a dream I'd had for seventeen years. My husband and I came for a visit, and I always said I'd come back here some day for this." The antecedent of "this" I took to be "dream" and not our immediate surroundings. Tom had made "a shitload" in Marin County real estate before he fell dead from a heart attack, and she decided she was going to spend it here. Tom never cared much for traveling in foreign countries.

"Well, are you writing?" I asked mischievously.

"I'm writing a play."

"How's it going?"

"A little every day."

"What's it about?" I went on, relishing the chance to subject her to the torture I've received when I make the mistake of
telling a stranger that I write.

"It's about the inability to articulate one's needs and feelings and ideas."

I'd expected a TV-Guide twelve-word summary (pilot
undergoes plastic surgery and sneaks into China to rescue
a dissident physicist), what I normally give my idly curious.
She seemed so proud to be wrestling with such a demon that I
couldn't resist asking, "Is that a problem for you?"

"Yes." She brightened. I think she was beginning to enjoy
being interviewed. "I was very repressed as a child in Alabama,
and that's why I rebelled so much I was about the only girl
in my sorority at Millsaps who'd tell anyone who asked that I
smoked and drank and danced and even screwed. You'll hear
me say fuck sometimes. It's to convince myself I'm still alive
and kicking."

Of course, the danger in expressing interest in her writing
lay in being asked to read or to listen to this play, but Franco
spared us that by suddenly turning up the volume on the
radio and singing "Bom-ba-lay-yah" with the Gipsy Kings
while slamming empty chairs assdown on the cleared tables.
This was his way of letting us know we were to leave.

We accompanied her down the hall to her room, which,
it turned out, was next to ours. It took awhile. She dragged
one leg behind her and mashed one dead arm on the wall for
support. She was wearing white hose and thin, dainty slippers
despite the chill.

She wanted to keep up the conversation as we inched
along, which necessitated that she stop to gesture or merely to

emphasize something as she explained how she'd come to be here at Franco's. She said that when she first came to Rome two years ago, she'd stayed in five-star hotels and had had a nice apartment for a while in Trastavere, but around Christmas she started worrying about money. Now she was running out.

She accepted my helping her through the door to her room, though I knew that she negotiated this several times a day on her own. Her room was the size of a large closet, with a window that, like ours, leaked in light from the construction site. The walls were lined with huge steamer trunks whose yawning lids showed clumps of clothing being vomited onto the floor. There was a single bed cluttered with more clothing and cosmetics and a box of crackers, but no desk and no visible pen or pencils or paper. I personally could not have written a single word worth reading in that cold small closet. A taint of urine nicked the air.

The crackers made me wonder suddenly where she ate lunch or dinner, given her lack of mobility. The *pensione* was officially only a bed-and-breakfast, but did Franco give her another meal? I didn't ask.

I found out later that night, though, when she knocked on our door after we'd come in from dinner, weary from a long day of sight-seeing. She was still wearing the green wool suit and beret and she had a 5,000 lire note in her hand, which she thrust at me when I opened the door.

"I wonder if you'd do me a favor," she said, lurching over the threshold. "If you go out tomorrow to buy more of those oranges, would you get me some? And bread? I think you said you were planning to buy some peanut butter, too, if you found it."

"Sure."

Marcia said, "Would you like an orange now?"

"Maybe to take back, if you don't mind."

I invited her to sit on the bed and offered her a glass of wine, which she accepted without any concession to the protocol that requires one to resist and be cajoled into acceptance.

"How'd the writing go?" I asked.

"So-so. Sometimes it's hard."

"Do you use a typewriter or longhand?" I'd heard the same dumb question a trillion times, but I'd asked not just to get a writer's revenge, but because her obvious affliction made me curious.

"I used to use that hand." She nodded to her left, which lay palm up in her lap.

"I guess it's tough to get around, too," said Marcia. This was an oblique reference to the stroke that had not yet been mentioned. I wondered if she'd had it before or after she left home.

"Oh, it's terrible. It takes me all day to go to the bank or the store. If I have to move someplace, I get terrified. I'm in a state of anxiety from the moment I leave one place until I arrive at another. I have to go up and down the platform of the train looking for a man who will carry my bags. When I first came to Italy, I had enough money that people were willing to do things for me, I could just wave *lire*, but now..." She shrugged.

"It was certainly brave of you to come here, alone, given your circumstances," said Marcia.

She chuckled. "My daughter said I was out of my fucking mind."

I nodded as if in sympathy for her having to endure the hysteria of an over-anxious child, but, truth told, if my mother were a widow who'd had a stroke and she'd decided to spend a few years living alone in an Italian cold-water *pensione* on the last of her nest egg, I'd be tearing my hair out, too.

"Franco's trying to get rid of me."

"Get rid of you?"

"I get in his way." She gave us a smile, but her dead side stubbornly held its own corner back. "He's afraid I'm going to croak and he'll have to deal with my corpse."

"He won't help you — shop for you?"

She shook her head.

"Is breakfast the only meal you eat here?"

"Yes. I go out now and then to the market for what I need."

I asked the obvious question, one that her daughter had no doubt posed many times: "Why don't you go back home?"

"America is full of bourgeois Republican fucks. I can't be an artist there."

"But your life is so hard, here. It would seem to me that if you were back home in California, you could devote your time and energy to writing instead of having to use so much of it struggling with the basics."

Her look pitied me. "Suffering is good for an artist's soul."

I let that pass without rebuttal and asked, "But don't you get homesick? If not for the USA, for where you came from, your town, you know, doctors and stores and friends and family?"

She carefully sipped the wine I'd served her in a collapsible camp cup.

"Never for a minute. My daughter's a bitch and she hates me. You know the best Christmas I ever spent was last Christmas. I'd been more or less evicted from my apartment. Somebody in my building told me about a nice hotel down on the Amalfi coast, and I decided to treat myself. But when I got down there, it was closing for the holidays. They let me stay in it, anyway. I had the whole hotel to myself. I hired a local woman to come in and cook for me." She was looking at the wall, as if at a movie screen. "It was actually pleasant."

She took another sip of wine. "Besides, I have to have this distance from America to write about it."

Ah, that telling "besides!" *Besides* offers the listener multiple reasons to pick from, meaning the speaker secretly suspects none could stand alone or that the real reason needs to be hid among false ones. *Besides* says *Pay no attention to that man behind the curtain.*

We rushed through breakfast the following morning in case she wanted to sit with us; we could excuse ourselves and say we were in a hurry to complete our whirlwind tour of Rome, and, "besides," we do need to go to the *alimentari*, also, no? It turned out that our haste was either unnecessary or efficient: we got away clear without seeing her.

But as if to fix our emotional compass as we two American tourists set out to do Roma, Franco ebulliently accosted us as we were leaving, giving Marcia one of his torso-clenching cheek swabs — "I love you, bella! Go away and have a good time! Come back soon!" Thinking he presumed we were checking out, I said, "We'll be back this evening, Franco!" and he chortled and said, "Too soon!" When I turned to go, he pinched my ass. I snickered at him over my shoulder, baring eyeteeth. I'm almost six feet tall, with a medium build, not particularly handsome, and was going on fifty years old, and this was the first time I'd ever had my ass pinched by man or woman.

The most pleasant part of the day we spent in the Farnese

Gardens on the Palantine overlooking the Forum. The sun was out, and in the gardens lilac and japonica were in bloom, and we found a grassy bower adorned with clover and daisies and dozed in the sun there after picnicking on bread, salami, cheese, water and wine. I kept thinking of Franco's pinching my ass. It gave me some insight into why women hate it. It makes you mad that somebody would surprise you like that and take such liberties to do you even such little harm (well, of course, it didn't really hurt, but still...) You want revenge, but the whole thing's been done in such a, well, jocular way that it makes your revenge seem an overreaction, like you can't take a joke. It wasn't sexual; it was political — Franco was an Italian writhing from his dependence upon tourist dollars who'd found an ingenious way of using eighth-grade grab-ass as a means of spilling his unhappiness on me. Now it seemed that his contempt for us was not a mask at all; we were just unwilling to recognize that we were seeing his true face because it'd be outrageous for him to hate us so openly. But there it was. And he relied on our need to deny it.

Blanche seemed to know it for what it was. And yet tolerated it. Endured it, anyway. I felt a little guilty about having deliberately bolted the breakfast table. She seemed lonely and eager for attention, and, of course, that explained both the guilt and the hurry to avoid her. To tell the truth, her absurd vanity about being an artist annoyed me. That collection of tired romantic cliches about writing — the need to suffer, the need for distance, the necessity of being an expatriate — seemed as crippling to any real achievement as was her stroke to walking.

She was once a beauty and was now supposedly writing a play: that spelled "actress" to me, and I wondered if the real drama wasn't her play-acting as A Writer. I thought she must have a high threshold for depression to live in that room and endure such difficulties. Maybe the "suffering" had a romantic aura; maybe it was a substitute for true artistic achievement, or maybe she considered it the initiation necessary for entry into the brotherhood.

Maybe this "longtime dream" was so intense and persistent that she couldn't even recognize that it had turned into a nightmare, and maybe she had too much pride to admit she was wrong.

Marcia had another take on it. "You know my friend, Janet, at work? She always tells me that her mother calls her for apparently no reason other than to tell her that she has stopped taking her heart medicine. Maybe Blanche is sticking it out here in Italy just to worry her daughter."

The terrible thing was that if she couldn't afford to go home and couldn't swallow her pride to ask her daughter for help, she'd literally limp along from day to day until Franco either booted her out or she "croaked," as she said.

Well, it wasn't my problem. I didn't even have what you'd call full information on the situation, and I'd be leaving tomorrow, anyway. But I was nagged by the idea that the relationship between Blanche and Franco was faintly similar to the one between an abusive husband and his wife and that she was psychologically stuck in this "marriage" the way such a wife was. To stand up to him, she ran the risk of being put out onto the street.

On the way back to our room late in the afternoon, we stopped into an *alimentari* and found the items Blanche had requested. Her 5,000 lire note wouldn't cover the sum, and, somehow not to my surprise, when I knocked on her door and handed over the bag of oranges, bread, and peanut butter, she didn't ask me what the total had been, and I didn't volunteer it. I'd been induced to make a donation.

Later in the evening, someone knocked. We looked at each other. We were reading in bed fully clothed under the covers. Moments earlier, Marcia had gone to Franco to complain that it was colder in our room than it was outside, and he'd said, "So go sleep outside." Possibly, the knock was Franco responding to our plea for heat, but I suspected otherwise.

I got up, went to the door, and cracked it open.

"I just wanted to say thanks again for the groceries." Bread or cracker crumbs were clinging to her sweater, and her breath smelled of peanut butter. I knew what she really wanted, but I merely stood filling the crack in the door and tried to look sleepy.

"You're quite welcome."

"I've been really selfish."

"How's that?" My hand was twitching on the doorknob.

"Well, I've told you both all about myself and my troubles and my aspirations and I haven't so much as learned your last names."

I told her.

"It was a manner of speaking," she said, as if my name were irrelevant. "I meant I want to... be interested in you. How can I be a writer without being interested in people? Surely you and your wife have things to tell a writer that would be worth hearing?" She shook a knobby finger playfully in my face. "I could put you in my play." I heard here some ancient echo of the "charm" practiced by Southern women, and if her smile hadn't been so torqued to one side, I'd have said she was simpering at me.

I decided on modesty. "Oh, no, not us, not really. But maybe by breakfast we'll have thought of something you could use."

We felt guilty about not inviting her in, so the next morning we paused at her door, thinking that we could at least escort her to the dining room, but, hearing nothing behind it after knocking, we presumed she'd already gone down the hall.

She wasn't in the dining room, however, and we lingered at the table waiting to take our medicine for neglecting her. By 8:40 she still hadn't appeared. We planned to check out following breakfast, so we could either slip away or make a point of saying good-bye.

"Maybe something's happened to her," said Marcia.

I got up and went down the hall. When I'd taken the left into our corridor, I saw immediately that the door to the bathroom was cocked fully open and that she was sitting on the toilet in a nightgown smoking a cigarette. Startled, I froze for an instant, not knowing whether to backpedal or avert my eyes and sail on by as if oblivious to her. Her gaze swung up, though, and I was forced to acknowledge my awareness of her.

"You okay?" I called out.

She waved vaguely and casually, then exhaled to watch the smoke plume toward the ceiling. You'd have thought we were office workers and she'd looked up from a computer to return a greeting.

"She's on the john," I reported. "With the door open."

"Maybe it's an exercise in shedding repression."

We laughed. But the longer we mused about it, she crossed

the line between harmless eccentric and mental patient. And we decided that if anyone close to us was in such a condition and situation, we'd want to know about it.

When Franco started clearing away our dishes, I said, "I see our writer friend didn't make it to breakfast."

"So?"

"So nothing, really, just that I think it's the only real meal of the day she eats. Or—?"

"I'm supposed to give her a special invitation?"

"Well, no. I know she must be a lot of trouble."

He didn't take this bait. He leaned over to grip the big bus tray by its handles. "I'm not running a fucking nursing home here."

"Oh, no, of course not. But she told me she has a daughter in California, and I wondered whether she was aware of her mother's, uh, difficulties here."

"Call her yourself. Be my guest."

A while later, we were at the front desk checking out with Augusta. We paid our bill, then traded the bolus of jangling keys for our passports.

Just as we were about to board the elevator, Augusta said, "He called the daughter."

Thinking we'd inspired this, I beamed and said, "Really!"

Augusta's languid, offhand wave said it happened long ago. "She said it's her bed."

The Folks
at Café d'Angleterre

A longing to be known becomes a potent force

Only moments ago, just before we were served our *creme caramel*, something important happened at our restaurant, the *Café d'Angleterre*.

We've been thinking and speaking of the *Café d'Angleterre* as "our" restaurant, but we've suspected in our heart of hearts that this doesn't mean much more than what it means to say that here's "our" bus stop or "our" bank.

Well, maybe a little more than that. I'd like to think so, anyway. I mean we do feel a loyalty to it that would inspire us to defend it if someone, another American tourist say, complained about the food or the service. Not that there's anything to complain of, but you know how some people are when they travel; if something's not what they're used to, then it's something to gripe about.

If I heard somebody running down "our" *Café d'Angleterre*, then I'd feel superior and smug, and I'd most likely give him or her a lecturette on how to appreciate things quintessentially French. (Though it's called *Café d'Angleterre*, there's nothing

English about it — it's in Nice's *Rue d'Angleterre*.) I might mentally sentence this person to a lifetime of dinner at Denny's or the International House of Pancakes. If he or she snickered or shuddered because of having to sit too near the old dwarf in his bow tie and the tiny and ancient dowager in her little mink stole, I'd know that this person's idea of ideal dining companions is a room full of others like him or herself — mirrors, in other words — and I'd honk that Gallic "Humph!" through my nose. As for how patrons are allowed to feed their lapdogs while they eat or fire up those stinky Gauloises and their cigars and pipes no matter where they're seated, what can I say except, "*C'est la vie!*"

We would never recommend our *Café d'Angleterre* to anyone. We want to keep it for ourselves. Last thing we'd want would be a bunch of people like ourselves in here looking around and being charmed or offended, and the next thing you'd know it'd be listed in *Let's Go* and gaggles of loud Tri Delts on spring break would crowd out the regular patrons. *Café d'Angleterre* is "our" restaurant partly because we're the only people like ourselves here.

Café d'Angleterre has what you might call "banquet seating" — long tables arranged in a horseshoe with the opening pointed toward the kitchen, and long tables running parallel along and to the walls. Right now Marcia and I are lunching across from one another in the bow of the horseshoe. Two fellows here together are seated one apiece next to each of us. They're not regulars. Not that we know of, anyway. We've never seen them in the dozen occasions that we've had lunch here, and "our" waitress (the cafe only has one, with help from the proprietress) doesn't treat them with familiarity. They talk across the table in growly Provençal French, tagging on a gutteral "guh" to many words ending in "n," so that *"demain"* becomes *"demang."* They've got sweaty bandanas tied around their necks and huge tanned hands with filthy nails and knuckles that look like warts the size of mushrooms. Their manners are appalling. One blew his nose on his hand and wiped his palm on his thigh. They slurped their soup and ate their *lupin* with sauce drenched dirty fingers, then sat and sucked on each and every bone with lusty smacking noises such as boots make lifting out of mud. They're country fellows, I'm betting.

We outwait them, and when they leave, their tip is miniscule even for a *prix nets* meal, and I'm offended on behalf of "our" waitress, a very pleasant woman in her forties who always wears a black dress and a white apron over it. She wears her hair in a June Cleaver length and style. If she were in America, I think her name would be Evelyn. The first time she waited on us she had to baby us a little since we were trying out our French; we were ordering not a la carte but "Le Menu," what you'd call a blue-plate special, so we didn't know for sure what we'd be served and wanted her to explain.

We made a fuss over each dish, though, ooed and aahhed and grinned and pointed toward our empty plates to pantomime our satisfaction and we much overused our limited superlatives of praise: *"Bon! Tres bon! C'est superbe!"* all of which was true.

Of course, being so easy to please we ran the risk of the cook's contempt, but it made our waitress happy to serve us.

Point is, we tip pretty good, so she's come to recognize us and gives us a smile and a melodious *"Bonjour!"* when she comes to take our order. Likewise, the "Madame la Patroness" hails us when we come through the door. Not by name, of course — we're *"Monsieur"* and *"Madame."* She's about fifty or so, always wears a dress with quarter-length sleeves and low-heeled pumps and glasses on a chain. She greets almost every-one, and she's the one you pay on the way out, so if you show up often enough, we figure she's going to put you in her mental album sooner or later, the album labeled "my" customers.

We haven't been sure we're in that album yet, though after what happened just moments ago, we feel the chances get bet-ter with each day that passes.

We found our *Cafe d'Angleterre* by happy accident. Among the many wonders of Nice, France (not counting our *Café d'Angleterre*), is its many clean, cheap, and conveniently locat-ed laundromats. (Nice may be the capital of the *Côte d'Azur* to jet-setting film stars, but to us it will always be the City of Laundromats and "our" other little secret. Ball-park guess-ing would be 1 laundromat per 500,000 inhabitants in most Southern European cities; in Nice, it's 1 per 1,000.)

Our first morning in Nice, we found a laundromat near our hotel and merrily stuffed four washers with our long-dirty clothes — almost everything we'd brought from home except for what we were wearing, actually — then decided we could eat lunch while the washers were churning. But where?

Right across the *Rue d'Angleterre* at the *Café d'Angleterre*! The street's only about two skips wide, anyway, and we could come across between courses and move the clothes into the dryers.

Well, you know how you are when you're traveling in a foreign place and you're considering the act of entering a restaurant that's not authorized by any guide book or other traveler's recommendation? What you do is stand outside the plate-glass windows on the sidewalk feeling very foolish and uncertain, knowing the patrons and the proprietress and the waitress inside can see you shifting your weight from foot to foot and kind of debating with your spouse and also trying to surreptitiously peek through the window to see if anyone else is eating in here, and, if so, who? Priests and their families? A gang of thieves? The local chapter of the Rotary? Nazis? Will the food be edible? Affordable? If we go in, will we come out alive?

Most places post a menu outside to save you (and them) time and energy and to spare you the embarrassment of hooding your eyes with your hand and mashing your face against the window to see what might be on somebody's table.

Our *Cafe d'Angleterre* has a mint-green dittoed handbill taped to the window. On the handbill an amateurishly hand-drawn chef is holding up a banner with the name, address and phone number of the restaurant, and underneath this fellow, the copy reads:

Vous aimez une cuisine simple? légère? sans complication?

Sure, we love "simple" food, if that means "not fancy-schmancy." For "légère," I had to bear the embarrassment of digging my palm-sized dictionary out of my jacket, and the entry was none too helpful: lightness, nimbleness, frivolity, slenderness, levity. Joke food!? Weight Watchers salad bar?

Le Restaurant Café d'Angleterre vous la propose.

— *Cuisine faite par le patron.*

— *Nombreux plats due terroir et de Tradition Française.*

— *Prix nets.*

Okay, the owner cooked regional and classic French dishes, and you could get multi-course lunches for eight or thirteen bucks respectively, tax and tip included.

It was busy inside. Right off we didn't see any customers who looked like travelers, and that might have been unsettling had the place been empty, but obviously it was popular with the locals. Madame La Patroness stepped from behind the register and came around the end of the high zinc-topped mahogany bar on our right. She murmured, *"Madame, Monseiur,"* then gestured for us to sit across from one another on one leg of the horseshoe. Our waitress, Evelyn, came bearing small glass flasks of water (used *pastis* bottles) and two glasses, and we made nuisances of ourselves by asking questions about the menu. We were here at the height of the lunch hours, and, as I said, our poor Evelyn was the sole waitress. She was patient but her answers were not lengthy, and the menu was fairly clear. For ten bucks each, we first had fresh crunchy-crusted bread and a salad of crisp tender butter lettuce with a creamy herb and horseradish vinaigrette, then there were potatoes Dauphine, followed by a whole broiled trout with an herb sauce, accompanied by green beans, a *quarte* of *vin rouge*, mineral water, and for a finale, a coffee eclair with a caramel sauce.

While we waited between courses, we looked about. On the bar were lined a full rank of Ricard "51" bottles filled with water and a vast array of liqueurs and brandies and cognacs ready to be dispensed. The walls bore an unmistakably French appearance; they were papered with a busy, gilded design that looked vaguely *fin-de-siècle* (whore-housey), and large mirrors were hung like so many paintings at eye level.

Next to Marcia sat a middle-aged dwarf in a ratty tweed

coat, bow-tie and spectacles. Next to him was an old woman so tiny and bent with osteoporosis that her highly powdered nose was almost pressed to the table. She had a mink stole draped across her shoulders and hump. Immediately I thought of Katherine Mansfield's Miss Brill, of course, and that became her name to me. During their lunch, the dwarf kept up a running conversation in gravelly French with a third party, another elderly woman seated on the far side of the ancient woman, whom they utterly ignored as if she weren't hunkered right between them in the stream of their dialogue.

I gave a start when I saw the fellow in the suit come in. He was a dead ringer for my grandfather, known to me as Big Daddy. He gave Madame Le Patroness the three times check-buss customary in the South of France, and they chortled together for a moment before he started down the line of diners, shaking hands and stopping to chat with them. I thought for a moment he might be the owner, but he eventually took a seat along the wall, unfurled a newspaper with a snap, slipped on his glasses, and Evelyn brought him his carafe of water and wine.

We came back day after day for a while and discovered that the Dwarf, Miss Brill, and Big Daddy were among the most consistent regulars. Along about mid-lunch, a fellow in his early twenties who bore a faint resemblance to one of the Baldwin brothers would enter and kiss Madame, and she would chuck his cheek or playfully twist his ear. Then he'd go down the line and shake hands with other regulars, speaking their names, joking or chatting with them. He'd disappear into the kitchen for a bit, come out carrying a plate of food and utensils and sit in the back corner where a huge sideboard and hutch that held crockery and silverware stood along the wall. The Son, we thought.

Though we were often moved about, the regulars sat at the same places, the Dwarf and Miss Brill together (or only adjacent?) along the side of the horseshoe, Big Daddy with his back to the mirrored wall. I got the impression that there were reserved seats and general admission. We noticed, too, that while Evelyn brought us each a cylinder of flatware wrapped in a paper napkin, she brought the regulars blue-checked cloth napkins in tarnished silver rings from a stack visible on the hutch. I wondered how long you'd have to eat at *Café d'Angleterre* before you'd rate your own blue-checked cloth napkin in a tarnished silver ring, and who would bring the subject up when that first day came — was this by invitation only, or could one apply? Neither of us would dream of asking for one.

After several days in a row of lunching at *our Café d'Angleterre* I grew restless, even though each meal had been *Bon! Superbe!* and we'd come to feel comfortable here. But day before yesterday, I was wondering should we stretch our wings, try someplace new?

It seems we're always torn between the need for novelty and the need for the stability the familiar provides. Sometimes I'm plagued by the idea that I have a duty to myself not to settle for the easiest thing such as returning to a hotel or a restaurant just because it has become a known quantity and even when the best that can be said is that it caused no pain. Sometimes I mislabel my anxiety over the unknown and call it stimulation, seek it out, make a virtue of it. After all, if I wanted familiarity,

I could have stayed at home. So I often feel obligated to use my time and energy expanding my experiences.

But so few opportunities for familiarity exist if you're touring Europe afoot for six months and changing cities on the average of every three days that any such chance we find for the familiar is almost irresistible. We cling to such tiny scraps as letting our eyes linger on American brand names in the *mercados* and *alimentarios* and *marches*, then we lift the boxes of Kellogg's Corn Flakes and liters of Coke off the shelves and handle them simply to enjoy the sensation of having the familiar weight, the logos and colors, in our hands again. We duck into McDonald's not because we want to eat there but because we want to *be* there; we rationalize by telling ourselves that not every minute in a foreign country has to be spent having a foreign experience.

So — we are homesick. If we can't be at home, we want at least to feel at home. We want to belong somewhere. We feel a deep yearning to be known.

But I usually consider this something to shrug off, and in its place I put the value of doing something new — such as eating lunch at another restaurant and not at our *Café d'Angleterre*. Marcia is against such impetuous experimentation. Why take the risk? she argues. Why cheat ourselves out of another chance to eat at our *Café d'Angleterre*? She means not just that we'd miss a good meal but also that we'd miss a chance to carve ourselves a little more deeply into the groove there.

Bolstered by a glowing review of *Au Soleil* in *Let's Go*, I won the argument, and yesterday's lunch was eaten in a new, strange restaurant where half of the chairs were empty and the other half were occupied by tourists. Not surprisingly, the service was surly, the food overpriced and mediocre, and I had to top off my meal with an indigestible serving of crow.

Chastened, we have crept back to our *Café d'Angleterre* for our lunch today, where (punishment for our disloyalty?), Madame seated us beside those two awful fellows from the sticks who blew their noses on their hands and sucked on their rabbit bones.

Evelyn has cleared our plates — we passed on the rabbit and had roast chicken, instead — and we're languidly finishing our wine and water while waiting for creme caramel and coffee. We're happy to be back here at our *Café d'Angleterre* after our secret betrayal yesterday, and we're relieved to see that while we were away, nothing has changed: Big Daddy is still reading his newspaper at his place along the mirrored wall, and the Dwarf, Miss Brill, and the third party are engaged in their usual dialogue, though Miss Brill is curved over so far you'd think she was inspecting her sauce for foreign particles.

The door opens, and the Son comes in. He and his mother exchange a quiet *"Bonjour, chérie"* and three cheek kisses, then the young man begins making his rounds. He shakes hands with those along the wall, comes to Big Daddy, who puts down his paper to chat with the Son for a moment, then the young fellow moves to the horseshoe, greets the Dwarf, hails Miss Brill with a cheek buss, dittos the other woman.

Then he strolls along the line at the top of the horseshoe near us, clapping diners on their shoulders, kissing women's hands. First thing you know he's reached the places just vacated by Billy Bob (Guillaume Robert) and his *ami*, which puts us next in the line.

We look at him, not really expectantly, but perhaps with

the pleasant yet vaguely hopeful demeanor girls wore at dances in junior high school. We can see his mind working: he doesn't quite "know" us, but he does "recognize" us.

He decides that makes us eligible! He steps up to me with a grin, sticks out his hand, and I shake it. He shakes with Marcia, too.

"*Bonjour, bonjour!*" he sings. "*Comment ça va?*"

"*Ça va bien!*" we both warble in unison. "*Merci beaucoup!*"

Okay, I'll admit it wasn't much. And, sure, we'd said exactly these words maybe a thousand times in our French class while preparing for this trip. But this was a real-life exchange in the French language with a French person and not a classroom exercise. We've been here enough times now that the Son has admitted us (sort of) to the inner circle.

We've now got our eye on two of those blue-checked napkins, but we're not expecting anything real soon.

Foundlings

*When the glorious past
bumps up against the prosaic present*

The Gypsy girl selling Kleenex and butane lighters is as feisty and tenacious as a pit bull. She's not what we've come to see here in the *Piazza della Santissima Anunziatta*, but she's what we've been watching for well over half an hour. She hasn't noticed us yet. She's about twelve I'd guess, with long black hair, and she's wearing a pink sweatshirt with its hood flung back, a gray wool skirt, and blue stockings badly laddered on her calves.

She's carrying a big red canvas bag with a strap over her shoulder that contains her goods, and when she strides from one side of the square to the other on the prowl, stalking her customers, she swings the bag back and forth like a great big yo-yo, at ease with its weight, toying with the tool of her trade the way a cop might twirl his nightstick or a janitor his chain of keys.

The girl's method is a variation of those the charities use when they send you, unsolicited, a desk calendar or other marginally useful trinket then ask you to give a "donation" for it. She stays constantly in motion, striding (sometimes almost skipping) up to everyone who comes into the square from any of its four entrances — housewives carrying bags, students, tourists, businessmen and women, workers, secretaries. When they spot her bearing down on them, most nix her off with a scowl and the "no! no! no!" of crossed arms violently wind-shield-wipering the air, and she doesn't waste a second working on these — she'll wheel off to someone else.

She keeps bouncing from one vociferous rejection to another until she lands on somebody not quite alert enough to ward her off or someone like a tourist who has no idea what she's up to, and then, that's when she digs in. My wife and I watch as she scoots quietly up behind two young women hugging books to their breasts. She speaks to them from off their starboard stern, and when the closest one turns, the Gypsy girl is poking a packet of Kleenex into her face. When the young woman, startled, leans back to see what's being brandished under her nose, the Gypsy girl drops it so that it's wedged between the books and the young woman's breast.

They argue. We're not near enough to hear what's said — and it's in Italian, anyway — but the girl seems to be insisting that the young woman asked for the Kleenex and has it in her possession and must therefore pay for it, and the young woman is protesting that she didn't ask for it and won't pay for it.

A stalemate, then the students toss their hair and stroll away. Now the Gypsy girl acts outraged and screams something like "Thieves!" at the top of her lungs and looks about as if appealing to bystanders or to an authority. The young woman with the tissue still wedged under her books whirls, glares, and lifts the books away so that the packet drops to the ground. The Gypsy girl pounces on it, then she chases on the young women's heels as they scurry out of the square, hollering in protest that her goods are now damaged and dirty, shaking the packet in their faces. She then scoots around in front of them and blocks their escape out of the piazza. She argues loud and fast and with a lot of gesticulating back to the spot where she first accosted these two, and finally her prey relents, digs furiously into her own shoulder bag, then flings a coin to the pavement at their feet. When the girl bends over to retrieve it, the two young women stride out of the square, yelling what are probably racial epithets over their shoulders.

The Gypsy girl shrugs, surveys the piazza, sniffs the air. Near where we rest on the steps of the *Spedale degli Innocenti*, a man sits behind the wheel of his car parked to the curb. His window is open, and he's bent over while trying to position and strap his child properly into a car seat beside him. The child is fussing and wiggling. Naturally, the man's not aware of the girl's approach, and she startles him when she pokes her head into the driver's window and says, *"Signore!"* He jumps, twists his head about, his hands still occupied with the child's seat straps, and the girl blasts him with a two-gun fast-draw, butane lighter in one hand, tissue packet in the other. Since he can only shake his head no-no-no, she drops her goods right into his lap.

Another uproar ensues, though in this case, the girl's prey is distracted by his own howling baby. He tries for a moment to wave the girl off and start his car, but she hangs to the sill and yammers at him, pointing into his lap. Like the girl's other customer, he decides that appeasement is his easiest course (he gets there quicker, though), but he makes it clear that he only wants the lighter, shakes it in the air and tosses it onto his dash, and keeps trying to hand her back the tissue packet. She won't take it; she keeps on arguing, shaking her head. His child is still bawling and squirming. Cursing, he roots about in his pocket then thrusts a bank note out of the window. The girl snatches it, walks away.

Now he starts hollering — obviously he gave her a bill from which he expected change (the fool), and she's not giving it to him. He starts his car and wheels away from the curb to catch up to her as she strides across the square, but she sashays behind the equestrian statue of Grand Duke Ferdinand I in the piazza's arena, skillfully keeping the statue between herself and his car, swinging the bag nonchalantly and looking about for new marks as he comes tooling around the base in an effort to catch her. She strikes out for the doorway to the church for which the piazza is named, and he pulls up beside her, waving out his window, arguing, but to no avail, and eventually when they reach the piazza's exit to *Via Gino Capponi*, he gives up and advertises his failure with a squeal of howling rubber as he peels out of the piazza.

The fellow had picked up his child from the building on whose steps we're sitting. Apparently there's a day-care center inside. During the hour we've sat here snacking and studying our guidebooks, a dozen Moms or Dads or nannies have come in cars, on foot, or on bicycles and have gone inside alone and come back out with children in tow or in their arms.

The building's officially the "Foundling Hospital," or *Spedale degli Innocenti*. My Baedeker's Florence pages say that in 1419 the silk merchant and tailors guild commissioned Brunelleschi to build it as an orphanage for the *Innocenti* (Innocents), the word for abandoned children derived from

Herod's slaughter of the children of Bethlehem. "Mothers who wanted to bring their new-born babies to the orphanage anonymously could (until 1875) place them in a revolving wooden cylinder ('Ruota') at the end of the portico," a device like a Lazy Susan, half of which was inside the building and half out. The Baedcker entry also says the building "marks the begin ning of Renaissance architecture in Florence."

Under *Piazza della Santissima Annunziata*, the Baedcker notes that it's "Judged the most beautiful square in Florence," by virtue of the four buildings that form it (the church, the hospital, the *Confraternita dei Servi de Maria*, and the *Palazzo Riccardi-Manelli*). Aside from the equestrian statue, the piazza contains two fountains with bronze sea creatures by Pietro Tacca. However, sitting here looking at the piazza, I'm surprised at such high praise. It's a gray day, for one thing, and the piazza's floor is covered with oil-drenched sand, and several construction barricades corral off corners of the square and make a zoo for machinery: a backhoe, a front-loader, wheelbarrows and pickaxes, powder-blue Porto-let, dumpster igloo in a particularly bilious green.

We came mainly to see the blue and white terra-cotta rondels by Luca Della Robbia that decorate the loggia over our heads. There are twelve facing the piazza, one each above the columns that support the outer eave of the loggia's roof. In each rondel is a single cherubic babe, a "foundling," wrapped in what appears to be bandages but is actually swaddling clothes, and each is reaching out imploringly with its tiny arms. We were led here to take a look largely because we were enchanted by Luca's famous *Cantoria* we'd just seen in the *Museo dell'Opera del Duomo*, only a few blocks away. Originally placed over the doorway to the left sacristy of the Cathedral of Florence, this depiction in marble of a children's choir is full of humor and impish delight — Frederick Hartt says that the youths and maidens have "street child faces as winsomely commonplace as those by Fra Filippo," and the rondels presently over our heads proved to be as captivating.

It seems we've been swimming in depictions of holy childhood ever since crossing the border into Italy. It has come as something of a shock (not a "surprise," however, since reading prepared me) to see just how intensely the Catholicism of Southern Europe is fixed on Mary, her motherhood. Mary Before or At Conception (the Annunciation), Mary And the Infant, Mary Grieving: these are the subjects of literally thousands of paintings, drawings, and sculptures by centuries of Italian artists. The Holy Mother and Her Holy Child at the various stages of their lives. In Florence alone we've seen dozens of Annunciations illustrating the moment when the archangel Gabriel appeared before Mary to tell her that she was (or would be) pregnant. The artistic interpretations are richly various. Sometimes the angel has red hair and white robe (Memling), or maybe fuchsia wings and gold hair (Fra Angelico), or looks very zaftig with pink fleshy limbs and blonde curls, big cardinal-red wings with many feathers, peach-fuzzed face, bare arms and throat and a calf coyly revealed below the robe (that one by Pablo Callari e Bottega); he may be carrying a Madonna Lily (Bartolommeo della Gatta, et al), and he or it may strike various poses — often going down on one knee (Gherardo Starnina) or hovering about a yard off the floor, or bursting through the bricks on the wing (Tintoretto) like some artillery shell. He may be commanding, beseeching, patronizing, or beside himself with the pleasure of what he has to tell: *a child will be born unto you.*

Mary, who has been reading or praying or sewing when she gets the news, is variously pleased, awe-struck, fearful, grave, coy, or downright sullen in response. She bows her head and submits, presumably with gratitude (Fra Angelico), or maybe she sneaks a look outside into her garden, or she's flung back on her chair when that angel and those *putti* come exploding through the wall, or she demurely casts down her eyes, or strikes an attitude that's decidedly put-upon (Simone Martini, in the Uffizi).

When the Christ child's born, the two of them sit for a hundred thousand portraits. As part of the course work for her master's degree, Marcia took a seminar in Italian Renaissance art, and she's got a very thick packet of cards in her jacket pocket that contain notes about these portraits. You can read therein how scholars have broken these illustrations down into such categories as No Bare Breast, One Bare or Two, With or Without Nimbi, Nursing or Non-Nursing Babe, and Chin-Chucking Child.

This piazza — with its church of the "virginal annunciation" and the *Confraternita dei Servi di Maria* across from the foundling hospital — seems like a theme park dedicated to the elevation of mother and childhood. Getting saturated in this sanctification of conception, of birth, and of childhood makes me see the Italians a little more clearly. I wax sentimental: I picture those hapless women who (until 1875) for whatever agonizing reason decided to slip into this piazza in the dead of night and steal along the shadows under the loggia to the far end, where they quickly and as quietly as possible laid a

swaddled bundle in the "Ruota" and gave it a turn before dart-
ing away in tears. How hard that must have been, how many
sleepless nights must have come before this one!

Across the piazza, in front of the loggia of the *Confraternita
dei Servi di Maria*, the Gypsy girl is trotting alongside a young
man on a white Vespa and waving a lighter in his face, but he
gives his wrist a twist and spurts away from her. Then we see
an old woman in a black coat and a grey head scarf approach
the girl and buy a packet of Kleenex voluntarily.

The afternoon is ticking by, and it must be near the hour
for the day-care center to close because within a short time
several adults are converging on the door behind us. A woman comes out with a toddler in her arms and carries him to
her bicycle, where she lowers him into a child's seat over the
back wheel and straps, buckles, hog-ties him into it. She zips
his fleecy suit up against the chill. She tugs his little woolen
watch cap down over his ears. There's a big wicker basket
draped from the handlebars, and inside it is a grocery sack.
The woman reaches into the sack and pulls out a bun the size
of a baseball and gives it to the toddler to suck and gnaw on.

Just as the woman is about to mount up on her bike and
move out, here comes Little Red Carrying Bag trotting from
all the way across the piazza, and no sooner has the mother
straddled the frame and straightened her skirt than the girl
is right there in front of her. They're near enough that we can
hear, but we can't understand. The girl's features are more
clearly visible to us now, and I knock another year off her age.
She's got dark, dark eyes and brows, a cherub's cheeks, and a
pouty mouth you might see on a sixth-grade bully. She looks

a trifle portly; she's still at that age when a girl's waist is as big as her bust or hips.

She is thrusting packets of Kleenex into the woman's face, but the woman declares, "No!" in an emphatic way unmistakable in any language. When the girl looks as if she's going to drop the packets into the grocery bag, the mother thrusts forward and covers the opening with her hands, shaking her head.

Then the mother says something like "Ah!" as if struck by an idea, raises her index finger (hold it a sec!), and while the Gypsy girl looks on, momentarily baffled, the mother roots about in the grocery sack.

She brings out another bun and offers it to the Gypsy girl. The girl's eyes dart to the toddler and back to the mother, and now she says "No!" But oddly enough she doesn't seem to mean she won't barter, she means she won't take charity.

Instead of pressing her case, she turns and begins strolling in our direction. The mother pushes herself off on one foot and rolls up behind the Gypsy girl, rides beside her for a moment, holding out the bun, talking to the girl, but the girl haughtily turns away, goes "puh!" in contempt.

She's coming this way but she's not looking at us yet. Between us are several parents still milling on the loggia with their off-spring. I picture the girl in swaddling clothes, her mother putting her on the "Ruota" in the dead of night and giving it a turn, but soon as she's in the building, the girl sticks out her bambino's tiny leg and gives herself a kicking boost back outside. If she makes it down to us, I'll buy both tissue and a lighter in honor of her winsomely commonplace face.

We Teach the French
About Texas Chili, Sort of

Culinary hubris leads inevitably to humiliation

I don't know about anyone else, but I personally get a little tired of the French always claiming they've got a monopoly on good food.

That's why we took up the gauntlet they flung down when they invited us to bring something "native" to an international potluck dinner. It was supposed to be in the one-world spirit of sharing, but if you know the French you also know that this was really like the Pillsbury Bake-Off: someone was going to win, and they figured on nabbing the prize.

I'm exaggerating only a little. What happened was this — before we left home for a six-months' tramp about Europe, we arranged to stay for two weeks in a village west of Avignon to work with other volunteers restoring medieval chateaux in the area. The brochure mentioned this aforementioned pot-luck supper. Since we were traveling without a car and with only one totable bag apiece, we struggled to think of what we might take with us to fix on this International Pot-Luck Night months down the road.

We'd bought some *Hell-fire! That's stuff's hottern blue*

blazes! chili powder on a recent trip to Santa Fe, so we decided that we could probably get tomatoes, ground beef, onions and beans when we arrived, and we'd make a batch of bonafide Texas chili. (Are you going to argue with me about the beans?)

All we needed for the native touch was the chili powder. We took about a half cup of it and wrapped it in a Ziplock bag doubly secured with swatches of masking tape, then Marcia wedged it down into the bottom of a side pocket in her suitcase. We ignored it and went merrily about our business for the next three months across Spain, Portugal, Italy, Switzerland, and parts of France, never touching it as we packed and unpacked, washed and dried our clothes, etc.

When we got to the village of *St. Victor le Coste,* we found out that the international potluck night had been scotched, but when we told our French hostesses, Simone and Irene, about our original plans, why then they insisted that we cook a batch of this genuine Texas chili for the 18 volunteers on the project.

Among the many, many pleasures of this two-week stint were our meals. (One student wag dubbed this whole enterprise as "All you can eat for $225 a week!") We were staying on a rocky hillside in old, thick-walled medieval dwellings that had been restored and which were separated by winding cobblestone paths. We all ate at a long, battered board table that the organization's founder, Henri Ginoux, had salvaged from a river barge, and this table was set on an arbor-shaded terrace overlooking Provençal hills and vineyards and the rest of the village down below. We had family-styled meals prepared under the guidance of the primary cook, Irene, who had a postgraduate degree in history and a very typically Gallic contempt for both the American palate and what she considered to be our "lack of respect for the food," as can be recalled from my earlier account of the Rape of the Cheese.

Most of the day we "international volunteers" were occupied with building walls or laying tile floors or clearing out old ruins, but at least once a week each of us had kitchen duty under Irene and her sous chef, Marta, a Chilean expatriate. Neither Simone nor Henri ever deigned to speak a word of English (this was ostensibly pedagogical), so we had to lumber along in touristese, but when Irene heard the news of our willingness to make chili, she said, "Thot ees good!"

The outfit was on a shoestring budget and there were always signs during the meals that an ingenious economy had been practiced in utilizing leftovers, never once to the detriment of the taste or presentation of a dish. (Okay, yeah, they are good at this, but don't you wish they'd shut up about it?) We told Simone that for twenty people we'd need about four pounds of ground beef, three to four giant tins of tomatoes, and a couple huge canisters of pinto beans — well, pintos for Texas chili, kidneys for the inferior Yankee version. (Frankly, we were guessing about the quantities. Six to eight servings was the upper limit for our usual recipe.)

Simone looked worried. It was a lot of stuff to her, you could tell. But she approved the purchase, and we went into Beziers with Henri on the regular shopping trip to get the ingredients.

In the meantime, word had spread that the Texans were going to make some Texas chili. I think it was the adjective that most piqued people's interest. They knew we claimed Texas to be the spiritual home of the stuff, and we began hyping our batch long before we ever got into the kitchen. *No, this ain't gonna be none of your mealy-mouthed, limp-wristed Yankee crap! This here's gonna be TEXAS chili, son!* Someone sidled up to us on the job site days before we were to serve it and said, "Uh, listen, do you think I'm gonna be able to eat this chili? Will there be something else for people to eat? I break out in hives if I even smell a hot pepper." We said, *Har de har har, matey, walk that damn plank like a man!*

And of course everybody from Tours to Timbuktu had a story about chili eaten in Guam or Leningrad or Botswana that was the best any human had ever tasted. One woman from Minnesota was a vegetarian, and she asked us if we would make a separate batch of "vegetarian chili." Huh? I said. "Vegetarian chili," she repeated. I tried my best not to laugh, but I told her that she could "pick the beef out of it," and thought, Good honk! Good luck!

Oh, we were smug. We decided to make it a day ahead so it could marinate in itself. We said the way we make it in Texas you go to your nearest gourmet grocery and buy dried cow-chips to cook it over in your back yard, then when that old black pot's cooled off a bit, you lug it off into the closest mesquite thicket, where you let it sit covered overnight. You put the lid on tight enough to keep out bugs but loose enough to let it take on the natural tang that's riding on the air: crude oil vapors, faint snatch of *corridos* or a whang of *mariachi*, a whiff of saddle leather and horse apples; then, after a night out on the prairie, all it needs is for the cook to hold an iPod playing Bob Wills' "I'm A Ding-Dong Daddy From Dumas" over it for a minute or two.

Obviously we'd have to skip some steps, we said, but we could give it that 24-hour lay-over. So we took kitchen duty the day before the due date, and, after lunch was served and we'd cleaned up the dishes, we assembled our materials and were ready. Irene walked home for her two-hour break before dinner, but Marta stayed to watch because, she claimed, she wanted to learn how we made it. (I suspect Simone ordered her to stay to make sure we didn't damage the kitchen.)

Things went smoothly through the early stages. We chopped several onions, browned all that meat, opened up the tins of tomatoes (they were big as snare drums), added mucho garlic and salt, and then we put everything in a ten-gallon vat on the stove to simmer.

Marcia went to her suitcase and retrieved the carefully sealed bag of chili powder from Chimayo. We opened it and debated how much of it should be put into the pot. We decided to use the whole shebang. We dumped it in. We figured that if it wasn't painful, it wasn't chili.

It cooked for an hour or so, then we decided to sample it. I took a spoon, dipped it, brought it out, tasted. What hit my tongue was — Ground roaches? Snake dookey? Anti-freeze? — and I instantly spat it onto the floor.

"Jesus Christ!" I yelled. "That's horrible! It doesn't even taste like food!"

They didn't believe me, of course. Marcia pa-tooied hers right into the sink. Marta tried it, screwed up her face until tears were squeegeed from her eye-slits, and said, *"Jabon?"*

Yeah? It did taste like, well, soap! Tide or Oxydol. It had a very heady, floral stink, and there was an overpowering chemical afterburn that completely obliterated any other taste. It wasn't even remotely *picante*. You couldn't taste meat or tomatoes or garlic, or onion or salt or the chili powder. All you could taste was soap.

The only explanation was easily arrived at but difficult to accept. Along with the carefully and tightly sealed bag of chili powder, whose taped wrapper had every iota as much integrity when we unwound it on this day as it had had when we packed it, we had also placed in close proximity several equally intact packets of laundry soap for hand washing. If there's a missing guidebook lesson in this, here it is — though you wouldn't have thought it possible, the floral bouquet in which that soap is saturated had communicated itself through four hermetically sealed layers of plastic and had come to reside in that chili powder.

Our chili was absolutely, unquestionably and comprehensively inedible. Not the "Oh, I'm so sorry it just didn't turn out the way it usually does" inedible of the cook fishing for a compliment — no, this crud would poison an alligator or a great white shark. Not even a goat would be tempted by it. We had wasted four pounds of ground beef, the tubs of tomatoes, the beans. Worse yet, now someone would have to dream up a new menu for tomorrow's lunch and go buy supplies for it. And all our fellows from Italy and America and Finland and, last and far from least, the braggart nation of France, would see these Texans get their comeuppance.

I said, "Well, we're just going to have to dump this crap out." I didn't want anybody else (such as Irene!) coming along and not taking our word for just how awful it was — so long as they didn't actually test it, they would imagine we were exaggerating out of modesty or a misplaced sense of perfectionism.

Too late. Marta said, "*Está Irene.*" Irene was almost at the door, and Marta added, *Tell her nothing. Let her try it.* I thought, well, okay, but fat lot of good that'll do.

"*Êtes-vous pret?*" she asked, smiling at the steaming bung of donkey puke atop the stove.

"*Oui,*" said Marta slyly.

Irene stepped up to the pot, dipped in a spoon, licked delicately at its tip. She cocked her head, frowned slightly. "Hmm," she commented. She continued to roll her eyes as if looking inward to see just how this chicken-coup soup was arranging itself on her palate. "*Étrange goût.*"

Strange taste, indeed! "*Comme savon?*" asked Marcia.

"*Oui!*" she said happily. "*Comme savon, exactement!*" She took another taste. "*C'est bizarre, eh?*"

Spellbound, I watched her try another sample. The most astonishing thing was how she seemed, well, *interested*, in a scholarly sort of way, in this aberration. She kept describing how the taste hit the palate in a brash burst of vile peculiarity, then there was a lingering aftertaste of piquant spiceyness (the chili powder, I guess). To hear her analyze it, it was a little as if she presumed that soap was part of our recipe — these Americans!

We moped and moaned and explained to her what had happened. We sobbed, groveled on our knees to beg for forgiveness.

To Irene, though, this was merely a challenge. She had some ideas, she said. First off, she dumped a bottle of the local red into it, then she walked outside and returned with a small thyme bush and a batch of rosemary the size of a Christmas wreath, and these she dumped into the vat. She added salt, a lot of salt.

I said, *Throw it out! It is a chili without hope!* But she said maybe the soap smell and taste would cook off.

An hour later people arrived for that night's dinner, the menu for which, fortunately, hadn't included our chili. Meanwhile, we made a pact not to explain or to apologize in advance for the swill we'd serve them at lunch tomorrow.

People were curious, though. *How's that Texas chili coming?* they asked. *We're looking forward to some of that authentic Texas chili. Real Texas chili, such as you Texans are fond of bragging about, as is the wont of you Texans.*

We said, *Uh, well, it's coming along okay. But you know, this will probably be a variation on the real thing, what with having to use local products and all, different pots and pans, you know how it is.* And then I'd go into the riff about the mesquite thicket and the indigenous vapors of the night pastures, etc.

On into the evening, we cooked it. We hovered over the pot and prayed, murmured incantations (*remember the Alamo, remember the Alamo*), hopefully hummed "The Yellow Rose of Texas." By bedtime it didn't smell quite so much like a flea-market perfume, but the taste was still unsurpassingly horrific.

I dreaded tomorrow. I got the impression that Simone and Irene were fully prepared to serve this barfy goop for lunch regardless of the taste — after all, it wasn't their nation's cuisine whose reputation would be devastated, and, as a matter of fact, maybe these smug frogs would love nothing better than for us to have to eat our own god-awful cooking, just like we were a bunch of Englishmen.

In the morning, Marta gave us the good luck sign when we left for work. She was going to let it simmer another four hours or so. All morning long I endured comments about the upcoming chili. *Boy, am I working up an appetite for some of that fine Texas chili!* some said. We said, *Well, it's a little different.*

Don't expect too much from it. Don't judge it too quickly. When people started getting suspicious, we had to clam up.

When we got back to the village for our usual two-hour lunch and rest period, we came down the walk toward the dining terrace, and Marta sidled up and murmured, "Ok." We went into the kitchen to help ladle this slop into serving bowls. Irene said that it was better now, that cooking it so long had burned off a lot of the floral bouquet.

I tried it. It bore not even a remote resemblance to chili from any known region of the Planet Earth, but at least it did seem to fall within the category of edible substances. It tasted like a cooked-to-death spaghetti sauce, flat and bland — it was to the tongue what beige carpeting is to the eye — with a distant hint of rosemary.

People said that it was good. I thought they were lying, but Simone's husband, Henri, he ate three bowls. He thought it was something he'd never had before.

"I'm glad it's not too hot," somebody said.

"Glad you like it," I said. "We had some help." And here I slyly ta-dahed to hand the dubious credit off to Irene.

"Mais non!" she crowed. *"C'est un chose Américaine!"* Of course by "modestly" disclaiming a role in the dubious success of the dish, she also sidestepped the blame for its utter lack of taste.

But there was no hiding from the truth — she knew we knew she'd performed a miracle. The score was Chef from France – 1; Chefs from Texas – zip.

Night Train

A new experience unearths an old memory

This phrase conjured images of Garbo as a dispossessed countess peering out her compartment window into pitch-black countryside, her troubled face, half-hidden by her hat, reflected back into the camera; you saw a small revolver being tucked into a purse by a red-taloned hand, and another, swarthy hand pilfering a sheaf of documents from a valise; the Orient Express and suspenseful frontier checkpoints with SS men in monocles, and for sure there'd be a bar car where men in fedoras and women in white gloves drink cocktails in stemmed glasses while smoke from their cigarettes makes milky light swirl around them like a genie's dreamy cloak.

I knew not to expect anything of the kind on an ordinary overnighter from Geneva to Nice, but boarding it I was as excited as a ten-year-old on his first plane ride. Even after four months of trekking, there was still this one eagerly anticipated experience left to complete my tourist merit badge, and when I wasn't imagining a collage of movie scenes, I was replaying warnings from travelers — everybody knew someone who knew someone who'd been hijacked, hoodwinked, badgered, buggered, peculated, rooked, plucked or fleeced while en route and snoozing in the dark. Here, for instance, is a note from a guidebook called *Europe By Train*: "Our advice to eurorail insomniacs is to have a heavy meal before the journey, take some ear plugs, and don't hold back on the local vino. A couple of years ago, however, many travelers on Italian trains accepted the 'hospitality' of their fellow travelers in the form of doped orange juice and other drinks, and woke up many hours later to find they had been robbed. These incidents, which were widely publicized, unfortunately gave others the same idea...."

Fellow travelers had likewise offered up a compendium of hints and tricks, depending upon the configuration of the sleeping compartments. My wife and I did and did not want a compartment to ourselves, really. For me, at least, sleeping in the same tiny space with a foreign stranger was in itself a novelty beyond the fact that the space might be in transit between two cities. But we'd decided for once to go first class, which meant only that we'd share with two others instead of four.

Our night train was to depart Geneva at 11 p.m., already past our bedtime. We found the right train and car that matched the numbers on our ticket without trouble. We found our compartment empty and readied — each of two upper and lower bunks held a neat stack of linen: a pillow, a single sheet sewn like a sleeping bag, and a blanket.

By now we were ready for anybody's bed anywhere. But the second I'd stepped up to board the car, the electric tick of adrenaline struck up in my veins and temporarily drowned out my fatigue. Giddy with exploratory curiosity, we spent several minutes pulling open any hatch that had a latch, anything with a knob or handle that looked like a cover or door, peering into nooks and crooks. Marcia decided she wanted an upper bunk because it would probably be warmer and more private, so she climbed up using the built-in step mounted on the wall. I handed up her bag and she shoved it onto a luggage rack.

"Hey, there's all kinds of little bags and pouches built in for your stuff up here," she said.

"I've got those, too." My lower bunk was as compactly engincered as a submariner's closet, with shelves and nooks and hooks. We spent a few minutes stowing our gear, digging out our ditty bags. This all reminded me of being in our mountaineer's tent and getting settled for the night, laying out the flashlight, the canteen, the knife.

"Are you still going to sleep in your clothes?" she asked.

We'd debated this; I said I wasn't going to change from street clothes to what the department stores might call sleep wear, and Marcia said she was. For me, ever on the alert, it was a matter of being ready for any confrontational possibility; I didn't want to be accosted by anyone while in my underwear.

"I don't know. I'll wait and see what happens. When are you going to change?"

"I don't know." Her face, upside down to my eye, popped around the curve of my ceiling, the upper bunk. "How do you like yours?"

"It's neat." I was lying on my back with my hands under my head. The bunk was almost too short but to my back it was nicely firm. "Is it warm up there?"

"Toasty." After a moment, she said, "I hope nobody else comes. You think we should turn out the lights and latch the door?"

"I don't know. There's one more name on the reservation

card outside the door." I looked at my watch; 10:35. I could hear other passengers coming down the aisle, clumping, knocking their luggage against the walls, muttering and talking.

"You think I should change now? I'm thinking that if we wait, the toilet will be crowded."

"Why don't you just change up there?"

"I have to go to the bathroom, too."

Our talk sounded trivial and mundane to my inner ear, but oddly jittery, too, like some kind of supercharged inanities. We were nervous and we didn't know what the deal was, the usual practice, the standard regimen. (I was about half angry with my parents' generation of Americans who'd made train travel on my continent only a historical oddity and so had left me with no legacy of how to act.) Though no one was present to sneer at us, we still feared doing something stupid and wanted to be taken as cagey vets, or at least not to be taken as fools. At the moment, we were lost because we couldn't follow our habit of looking about and spotting the person who appears to be the savviest and imitating him or her.

She gathered up her sweats and ditty bag, climbed down and went out the door. A few moments later, the door slid open and a young woman dressed in black slacks, a blue wool sweater decorated with white snowflakes, and a goose down jacket came in. She was carrying an overnight bag over her shoulder. She took one wary look at me lying on the bottom bunk. I smiled and tried to appear harmless. I said, "Hello." She said "Allo" back. For a moment she hesitated as if she might go elsewhere to find a bunk, then, when her eye swung up and she saw gear on the upper rack, she seemed to relax.

"My wife," I said, pointing upstairs. I wondered if I should repeat that in French.

Her response was to toss her bag up onto the bunk across from Marcia's and to climb up after it. She was wearing ski boots.

I tried to watch her without seeming to pry (is this possible?) while she immediately set to work: she removed her boots, spread out her sheet and blanket, shoved the goose down jacket and bag onto the shelf without opening it, shocked me by suddenly stripping off her sweater down to a white turtleneck, crawled into her sheet sack, turned to the wall, pulled the blanket up to her ear.

This all took thirty seconds. The swiftness and economy of it took my breath away — we'd spent thirty minutes it seemed debating whether to undress. I lay fairly paralyzed with self-consciousness, thinking that any sound I might make would be detected by that one uncovered ear.

Marcia came through the door with her mouth opening but she closed it when she saw in a flash my rigid finger pointing up to the blanket-humped hip of the stranger. With both of us reluctant to speak, there ensued many minutes of weird mime. Who the heck's that? Dunno. She asleep? Dunno. You have the tickets? Yeah. Give me some water. Okay.

Our silence made everything louder — howling unzip of a bag pocket as Marcia went to retrieve her sleep mask, the whoosh of a hurricane through palm trees as Marcia sat in her bunk and shrugged out of her trench coat.

Then the lights blinked, the train lurched and stretched its joints, popped its knuckles, and I saw the station wall sliding by. I sat up quietly in my bunk and scooted to the foot of it to peer out the window. I looked up into the top bunk to see if Marcia was ready for lights out, but she'd already mirrored the position of her silent twin across the aisle.

I turned out the compartment lights. I was fairly disappointed in the entertainment value of our fellow passenger; I'd hoped we'd get to interview whoever had signed on to run their lives parallel with ours, however briefly. But seeing the glittering ribbon of the Rhone from the railroad bridge as we crossed was a pleasure. I sat by the window for several minutes looking for similar cheap thrills, but I quickly grew weary. I'd been on the road for months.

I lay back on my bunk and drew my blanket up to my chin. The train had reached the outskirts of Geneva and was apparently up to speed. The joggling and vibrating bunk pressing up into my spine was as persistently annoying as a squadron of mosquitoes. That sadistic specter of unending consciousness arose to taunt me: *I don't care how tired you are. You will not sleep tonight!*

About twenty minutes out of the station, the door slammed open and the lights went up. The conductor — he seemed twenty feet tall from where I lay on the bunk — stood waiting to inspect our tickets. I don't know why train conductors always made me nervous — maybe I'd seen too many old movies in which fugitive heroes had to pass forged papers to escape over the frontier. But in any case, ticket inspecting always caused a tiny flicker of nervous energy through my system: we could be on the wrong train, in the wrong car or the wrong country, would be ordered in a language we didn't understand to do something such as report immediately to a dungeon.

Marcia sat up. The woman across from her rolled over and stared at the conductor balefully. She looked cross and rumpled, as if she'd been sleeping for hours. With the conductor coolly holding out his hand, she raised up on an elbow, reached into her goose down and got out her ticket. He punched it. She slipped it back, then turned over.

We had a special discount pass that SNCC, the French railway system, offered to married couples, but to use it required a photo ID you had to show to the conductor along with your ticket. I passed all the appropriate documents, and the very quantity of them seemed susceptible to suspicion. He looked from the photos to our faces, seemed satisfied, punched the tickets, murmured "Merci" and flicked off the lights as he left.

We went through Bellegarde, stopped at Aix-les-Bains and again at Chambery, and, though I heard people coming down the aisles, no one entered our compartment. Out of Chambery somewhere, I dozed off, because suddenly I was thrown fully awake by the train's stopping in the station at Grenoble. I looked out the window. The platform looked deserted. It was 1:30.

Then I heard rustling and footfalls in the aisle, and our door slid open. The light went on. A woman in a camel-colored overcoat and a scarf over her head entered carrying an infant wrapped in a blanket. The infant was fretting in little short gasps of exasperation and discomfort, waving its tiny fists and pedaling its legs in the air. The woman took a quick glance around, saw the empty bunk across from me, turned off the light.

She felt her way to the bunk. I smelled cologne, under it the faint acridity of ammonia. The woman went "shh, shh, shh!"

very quietly and soothingly, then I could see her shadowy outline as she leaned back, half-sitting, half-lying, with the infant at her breast.

She had no luggage. Soon we were sailing in the utter darkness through the tunnels in the mountains. The woman had a bronchial hack that she tried to squelch by coughing into the blanket. Now and then the child mewled, sighed, whimpered.

A woman with no luggage boards a train in the middle of the night. Is she running from someone, something? I thought of how tired she might be sitting up with the infant, how far she might be going. If it were only a short distance, that might explain the lack of luggage, but why not in the day, then? She might have stolen the infant. She might be running from a violent husband. Earlier today she heard that her father who lives in Nîmes had a heart attack? But wouldn't you take luggage, then?

Tantalizing though the mystery was, I awoke when the train stopped in Avignon and caught just a glimpse of her back as she scurried out of the compartment without turning on the light.

When the train started moving again, I lay fully awake with the sudden gift of a memory of going on a train from Tennessee to Florida with my mother. I was five, and we were going to see my grandmother. Our Pullman car — now no longer a basic component of American touring life — reminded me of a long narrow room with windows on two walls and rows of bunk beds arranged end to end, with curtains dropped from the ceiling to the floor for privacy. I had an upper berth, and once we were underway, I discovered that one wall of my little room was a shade that I could roll up. Now I had a bunk bed with a window onto the world, and I lay for hours on my side watching as the towns slid by my gaze. It was like dream-flying, the way my window was a huge eye cruising over the darkened land and sailing past a red-lamped, dinging crossing gate where a lone truck waited with headlights fuzzing in the mist, past outskirts where houses were dim but for lights in their bathrooms and on their stoops, past strings of red-bricked, sleepy-eyed stores, and once past a juke joint in whose rocky parking lot a man and a woman stood kissing in the V of an opened driver's door.

For almost fifty years, I'd only recalled lying in the dark and watching out the window, but lying in the dark decades later, I thought of this Nice bound train charging through the night with the calendar leaves superimposed over its racing engine, back past 1990 and on through the '80s, '70s, '60s, '50s, until it transformed into my night train to Florida in 1945, where that boy, that child long ago murdered by time, greeted his present with the lustful glee of the eagerly innocent. I saw the black porters spiffy in their uniforms ready the berths for sleeping. I could remember now how I walked the aisle agog to see full-grown people, absolute strangers, strolling about in bathrobes. A bearded man in his pajamas yawned and scratched his belly button while standing in the aisle, then he climbed through the curtain draped over the mouth of his berth, and a moment later, his hands came back out and he set his shoes on the floor outside; a woman came out of the toilet with Pond's cold cream shining on her cheeks and forehead, her hair in a net, wearing a chenille bathrobe, and a porter set a little ladder beside her berth so she could climb up into it.

I doubt I slept that night. When the lights dimmed, my ears

took over, and I lay eavesdropping while grownups coughed, murmured or called out to one another, rustled in their nests. Each thump or bump would send my finger crooking at the seam of my curtain and I'd peek to see who was doing what. Now and then we'd stop at a station and people would come through the car carrying bags, shushing one another, and once two drunk sailors suppressing giggles lurched along the aisle and brushed their shoulders against the thin cloth that was all that separated me from their unpredictable rowdiness.

The bearded man's empty shoes sat with many others in the aisle all night long. Now and then while the lights in the car were bright, I'd stick my head out of the curtain like a stage manager checking the house before the play opens, and I'd see those empty shoes littering the aisle. They carried an enormously portentous sense of the otherness of these strangers. Seeing these unknown adults in their night clothes, without their usual armor, their daytime, public masks, gave me the sensation that I was somehow invisible, a spy. It was as if all the world's houses had turned inside out and all the small and private acts of preparation for the humble act of sleep were visible. To my wonder, I saw that these adults and I belonged to the same species. A tiny part of the secret of what it meant to be grown up was suddenly made available to me, an unexpectedly lucky child.

In Praise of Stone

Humble materials take on a new perspective

In my remote southeast corner of New Mexico, most of the hamlets sprang up overnight during the oil boom of the 1930s. Their dirt streets were paved with crushed caliche or crude oil to stanch the dust. The land was prairie flat and almost as arid as a desert; mud was the only available indigenous material for building, but the Anglos who came West identified adobe with Spanish or Indian cultures. They were determined to hew both literally and figuratively to their own identities, so they rejected a centuries-old architecture that had evolved with the region. Instead, they imported pine and knocked up quick frame houses and stores and churches, usually one but occasionally two stories tall (picture the Dodge, Kansas, of lore, your standard Western movie set), and often stretched skins of galvanized tin across the studs and rafters.

Years later around World War II, some frame houses got a new dressing of asbestos shingles, and the more prosperous mainstream churches were rebuilt using brick. Often one-story with "modern" low-slung lines, they were similar in style

to the new, misnamed "ranch-style" houses going up in outly-
ing developments. Banks and schools went to a blondish brick
popular in the 50s, and some trees such as the Chinese elms
that had been imported in earlier years (any vegetation over
head-high was not native) grew to respectable, Eastern height,
and at last some of these communities had a semblance of so-
lidity and permanence.

But not much, not at least to my eye. Flying over the
stretches of the American West, you see just how little of it
has been settled. The landscape billows out beyond any human
dwelling and makes it flimsy and temporary. The Comanches
and Apaches who once hunted and raided on it lived in lodg-
es made of sticks and skin, and even the adobe buildings of
old Spanish settlements or the Pueblo tribes are given to ero-
sion and must be redressed periodically with a coat of mud.
(New "adobe" is cinder block coated with colored plaster.)
I've watched an old abandoned adobe church in Talpa, New
Mexico, gradually melt over the course of a decade now, and
each year that I drive past it on my way to Taos, the roofless
walls are a foot or so shorter, the corners more slumped and
rounded, and it's not hard to imagine wind and water breaking
it down into trillions of grains of sand, blowing and spreading
them until the church is no longer distinguishable from the
soil it came out of. Sand castle.

But every city in Europe is built upon a footing of stone.
On my first extended visit there, to my Westerner's eye, the
stone of Europe's cities expressed a daunting degree of age and
weight and firmness. On our first day in the Old World, my
wife and I got off the plane in a blurry rush, hurried down

Madrid's *Paseo del Prado* with our gear and checked into a hostal-residencia, then, free of our burdens and stepping light, we went out and turned into the nearest side street to explore.

What I'm calling *La Calle de Piedra* was narrow by American standards because when it was first carved out of the dirt we humans moved about on foot or on horseback or in carts and carriages.

More importantly, *La Calle de Piedra* was laid in cobblestones. I'd heard the word all my life. To say it was to conjure the clop of horses' hooves and the rumble of wooden wheels. I thought of capes and fog. Cobblestones were what revolutionaries ripped up out of the street to hurl at authorities from behind their barricades, and I never knew they were so uniform — the size and shape of small bread loaves — or that they were laid out so neatly like mosaic tile, often in a herringbone pattern, so that if you wished to use them as a weapon, you'd have to pry the first one up, but the others might then be lifted away from their ranks like so many brownies.

I was to walk up this same narrow street of cobbles in Toledo, in Malaga, in Florence and Avignon and Nice. And, later, I would watch men in Lisbon and Rome repair the design after work had gone on under the street — they carefully selected the loose stones that had been piled to the side for the excavation and fit them back into what I took to be their original places upon a bed of smoothed sand, like bricklayers setting a wall upon the ground.

The cobblestones of all my *Calles de Piedra* have rounded edges so that when their flanks were touching, the top surface has a quilted effect that leaves a small trough for draining and

makes humps and bumps you feel under the soles of American
running shoes or sneakers. Even with those troughs the stones
are slick in the rain, and dampness lying on them always takes
on a glossy sheen at night that reflects the lamps and gives the
street a glimmering, pebbled patina.

When you step onto the curb, you see that it's not one long
ribbon of poured concrete, but rather, like the street made of
cobblestones, the curb is also formed by larger loaves of stone
fit end to end and rounded up and over from the street to the
walk. Then you see that the sidewalks are also composed of
blocks of stone set and fit into place.

Rising from the walks on either side of the street are walls
of fitted stone that reach three stories or so. When you turn out
of the *Paseo del Prado* and into my *Calle de Piedra* in Madrid,
you stand looking at what your Westerner's eye sees as a hand-
built canyon of stone, with a dry, cobbled creek bed and gran-
ite banks and neat grey or ochre bluffs coming up from the
banks to box the sky above.

Walking this same narrow street of cobbles, this canyon of
stone, in Lisbon, in Florence, in Chartres, Assisi and Avignon,
Nice and Padua and Cologne, you can see that the individual
stones are veined, they have a skin, a texture of grit and pit, of
paint, of blood and skid marks, rain-washed soup stains; they
are mortared with lichen and spit, oil and wine and printer's
ink, smears of bread and excrement; they are etched by acid
rain and carriage wheels and a million broom straws whisked
across them — a bio-archeologist might scrape the top layer
away and read a civilization's long history under a microscope.

Walking these streets of cobbles, the canyons of stone, in

Sorrento, in Venice, in Cambridge and Zurich, Wurtzberg, Geneva and Nerja, Edinburgh or York, you wonder where are the quarries all this stone came from? How long have these walls, this street, been standing just this way?

Then you see that Europeans also built their homes of stone. Their banks, their railway stations, their hotels, the borders that mark off their parks and gardens and monuments. Their castles, fortresses — ancient cities boast stacks of stone still standing where citizens put up walls to keep invaders out before the birth of Christ.

They made the steps to the top and bottom of everything of stone; they used it to build their quays, their palace walls, the archways to enter or exit anywhere, for parapets and the frames of windows, used it for pillars and landings, their stoops and sills.

They built their churches out of stone. Whether the cathedral stands in Toledo, Sevilla, Rome, London, Chartres, Florence, Venice, Barcelona, Paris, or Cordoba, what made it remarkable to my Protestant Westerner's eye was the ponderous heft of the materials. If these churches were animate, they'd be the largest denizens of Jurassic Park, and when they walked, the ground would tremble. So anchored to the earth by sheer tonnage, the cathedrals of Europe express a paradox of intention: their builders sought the most permanent materials to build a fitting monument to God's eternal presence, his otherworldly and transcendent nature, and though the lines in their design point Heavenward, those tons of cold damp stone sometimes seem to be oozing back into the ground from where they've been heaved up (and Venice's *Basilica San Marco* is literally sinking), making the gap between Heaven and Earth only more painfully obvious: these great buildings have no where to go but down — their very weight demands it.

You could argue that if you wanted a cathedral that truly showed the nature of human life as opposed to heavenly immortality, a church that stood for the ideas of ascension and mutability, you might try making one from a soap bubble or a cloud.

And when I first saw the still-unfinished *La Sagrada Familia* in Barcelona, it struck me that Gaudi had perhaps been trying for such an effect in stone, with all those lacey-looking spires grouped around empty space like a battery of airy rockets aimed for the cosmos.

At other times it seemed a marvel to stand inside the huge grey domes and hunker awestruck under all those tons of weight being held aloft by little else than the stones themselves in amiable collusion with physics. Then, it seemed, rock was light, weighing nothing in the invisible palm of God's gravity.

Walking those streets of stone again and again, literally surrounded by work done by centuries of masons and artisans and architects, you see that the Europeans studied stone for so long they'd learned how to make it contradict itself. What keeps those slender flying buttresses miraculously aloft, and how can they be supporting anything but themselves? That big block of marble the size of your refrigerator looks hard and dense and heavy, but when it becomes Mary with her dead son draped across her lap, the folds in her robe look frozen in time but not in substance, and you imagine that if you could set the projector going again, they'd feel soft to the fingers. Or those

veins in David's hands. Or columns adorned with such un-
stone-like flourishes as figures of naked baby boys, leaves and
flowers and fruit, lizard-skin and feathers of gryphons — all
the mutable substances of the transitory world rendered life-
like in rock that would keep its form longer than that which it
represents but cannot precisely clone. In the Monastery of St.
Jeronimo in Belem, Portugal, you see the sugary rococo em-
bellishments known as Manueline, and stone webs connecting
pillars are carved to such delicate intricacy that the eye sees
them as lace doilies.

Walking those same stone streets in Merano, York, Bath,
Sienna, Evora, and Cordoba, you see that the stone comes out
of the earth with almost as many colors as we have in tropical
fish. The Europeans learned to use it like paint on the floors of
their cathedrals and mosques and palaces, where mosaics in
colored stone echo the narratives in the glass windows; they
used the color to achieve such striking effects as the red-and-
white peppermint horseshoe arches in the Mesquita Mosque
in Cordoba or the bold, green-and-white peppermint walls of
Sienna's Duomo, or the more subtle and enormously pleasing
confectionery arrangement of pink, cream and green marble that Giotto and Pisano used to build that edible-looking
Campanile in Florence.

Walking those same streets, you hear the stone say time
and age not only because the structures made from it have
been standing for so long, but also because using such stone
is a thing of the past itself. When your feet strike the stone or
your shoulder bumps a wall or you accidentally knock your
knuckles or your knee on a chunk of stony door frame, you

learn again the reputation of stone: dense, compact, hard, firm, rigid; substantial; stable, genuine, real, heavy, impenetrable, immovable, almost eternal.

Sometimes those qualities are oppressive, and that narrow cobblestone street you're walking up seems aloof and alien to your nature as a human. The stone has a way of soaking up the weather, and it will have a heavy, heartless look on a damp day when it absorbs the color of dingy grey clouds and oozes a cold sweat out its pores. If the weather's cold, the stone will feel still colder if you lean or sit on it, and it will leak wet black grit onto your hands and haunches in a most inhospitable way.

But it will likewise catch the light and hold the warmth of an afternoon sun right up to twilight. The mood of it then changes and the weight and firmness seem an anchor, protective, nurturing. You can press your shoulders or your loins against it and feel the radiant heat.

Walking up *La Calle de Piedra* on that first day in Madrid and telling myself that this was what Europe looked like, I was only testing, hypothesizing, but the image held true in every city we came to, and I came to see my canyon of stone in twenty different degrees of light.

Walking in Oxford's New College Lane just two days before leaving for home, I made the last mental sketch of European stone. This little cobblestone street is walled by Hertford College and New College; the waning sun still struck the top of the tall East wall and the stone had caught the yellow light and held it. Spiced-mustard light, dusty dusky yellow, wine-yellow, apple-yellow light thick as warm candle wax. A small orange wildflower poked out of a chink in the wall, and overhead, boxed by those ochre walls, the sky had paled to a powder blue base on which sailed galleons of British strato-cumulus.

The street was empty, and I walked in the middle of it to feel the rolling texture through my soles, thinking of those therapeutic bead-massagers. Then a bicyclist passed me from behind and the cobbles set up a jingle-jangle in some loose metallic parts. My heart soared, then got crimped in a pang of anticipated loss: this experience of walking up these streets would be what I would miss the most. More than anything else, what I wanted for a souvenir was a stone.

About the Author

C.W. Smith is the author of the novels *Thin Men of Haddam, Country Music, The Vestal Virgin Room, Buffalo Nickel, Hunter's Trap, Gabriel's Eye, Understanding Women, Purple Hearts,* and *Steplings.* He has also published a collection of short stories, *Letters From the Horse Latitudes,* and a memoir, *Uncle Dad.* He has worked as a teacher and journalist, and his short stories and articles have appeared in dozens of national magazines and periodicals, including *Esquire, Mademoiselle, TV Guide, the Utne Reader, Harper's Magazine Bookletter, Texas Monthly, Hemispheres,* and many others.

He has long been affiliated with Southern Methodist University as a Dedman Family Distinguished Professor in English. He has also worked as a musician, a newspaper reporter, a swamper on a pipe truck, a roustabout, a paper delivery boy, oil field hand, frame carpenter, and roofer. When he's not teaching and writing and reading, he likes to be in his kayak or on his bike accompanied by his wife, Marcia.

He has twice received the Jesse H. Jones Novel Award

from the Texas Institute of Letters; the Southwestern Library Association Award for Best Novel; the Dobie-Paisano Creative Writing Fellowship from the University of Texas; National Endowment for the Arts Creative Writing Fellowships in 1976 and 1990; the Texas Headliner's Feature Story award; the Frank O'Connor Memorial Short Story Award from Quartet magazine; the John H. McGinnis Short Story Award from Southwest Review; a Pushcart Prize Nomination from Southwest Review; Special Merit Award for Feature Writing from the Penney-Missouri Foundation; the Stanley Walker Award for Journalism from the Texas Institute of Letters, an SMU Research-Travel Grant, and an award for Best Nonfiction Book by a Texan in 1987 from the Southwestern Booksellers Association, and an award for Outstanding Book of the Southwest from the Border Regional Library Association. The Texas Institute of Letters named him a Lon Tinkle Fellow for "sustained excellence in a career," and gave him the Kay Cattarulla Award for Best Short Story of 2009. He belongs to PEN, The Authors Guild, Writer's Guild of America West, and the Texas Institute of Letters.

More information about C.W. Smith is available on Wikipedia and on his website: http://cwsmiththeauthor.com